#1 Best Seller - Getting Better

CHILLED DEMONS & CHEEKY HEROES

Finding Motivation in Midlife

Adam Senex

The Sky Is Not the Limit....The Mind Is.

" In a world in which most of us are preoccupied with externals – accumulating more stuff and building fake personas to fit every situation. I consider my task with my books to be as a messenger, someone that gives myself and others a gentle poke and to suggest that maybe there are other ways to think about things and more questions that need to be discovered and asked. Leading to yet more questions.

My task is to create an interesting, healing and pleasurable art out of self-examination and ultimately self-realization. This awareness made available to people who, like me, are finding themselves caught in the rigors and realizations involved in the process of growing up as mature adults in the second part of life, having assumed it would all get easier and that we were the finished article. Having no guide and holding ourselves and significant others to blame for being conned into believing we are fully matured but in no way prepared for what lies before us in the second part of life. Or for that matter what goes on behind our backs. If I can only manage to persuade one other person to look at what may really be going on in the world and inside of our hearts and minds, then I will have done tremendously well."

Adam Senex

X T Y X

ADAM SENEX

X   X   X

Contents

The Getting Better

All men and women are potential philosophers, although for some reason, the task and subsequent title has fallen to men more than to women. The first task of philosophers is to ask questions, the questions that we all have inside but never seem to ask. The second task is to try to find the answers to these questions. However, since the answers are only partial and they seem to raise yet more questions, philosophy both attracts and annoys us. The third task is to encourage all others to ask questions and seek answers for themselves. It is my hope that this book will seek out the inner philosopher in all of us, encouraging original thought and creativity and a refusal to accept any thought or idea handed to us as the defining truth on any subject.

We live in a time when we seem to celebrate dysfunctional misfits and idiots more than any person actually worthy of celebration, and we have malevolent celebrity politicians ruling our countries and much of the world. Appearing on television as fun and good personalities and then murdering thousands with their decisions in the name of "right". It's a time when appearances and impressive speeches have become more important than any depth of character. Speeches impress and then are forgotten. Merely achieving celebrity status makes you an expert on any subject. Celebrities full of their own self-importance seem to be convinced that they actually do have the one last objective truth on any subject. They act as moral guides for society through the social networking sites and a media network that will actually report any old rubbish any celebrity cares to utter, without prior thought. No sooner do thoughts leave their brains than they are aired to millions. Each thought is genius – not an opinion – the last word. A professional soccer player with a record for gratuitous violence is suddenly quoting Aristotle. Interesting. Another spokesperson for kicking racism out of football calls a fellow professional a racist name on the back of a very public court case. Why? Just because he didn't share his views! He dared to have his own opinion. He liked different thoughts. The professional as a role model? With millions of followers?

All things considered, I thought. Yes, that is what I do quite a lot. I think – in fact, I can't seem to stop thinking. How unique might it be for somebody not seeking celebrity status, someone having opted out as much as possible, to offer my unique individual opinions, thoughts, beliefs, and ideas on a wide-ranging and random set of topics, relevant to and affecting us all. Me, a Mr Nobody, voluntarily living life as lightly and invisibly as possible. This book, one in a series presented here and now for your information could be considered either the ranting of a madman or the wisdom of a life-tortured old sage, depending on your unique interpretation and individual perspective of its contents. More probably, you will see it as just thoughts, opinions, beliefs, and ideas to get your mind juices flowing before free thought becomes illegal, taxable, or we are distracted to such a degree that we entirely lose the ability to personally reflect. Or, in the worst possible scenario, until original thought becomes a skill that humans are no longer capable of performing. We are already implanted with much that we hold as our own thoughts. Think again. Future generations will evolve without such creative ability as free and original thought – unless, of course, we can do it in 140 characters or less! Before you even try it, I am sure a well-known professional sportsman or famous (for what?) celebrity has already tweeted the meaning of life. Think on. Enjoy the currently free process of personal reflection. If we do not learn how to protect, control and use our own minds for the benefit of the human race there will be others that will take control for the enslavement of us all. It is happening right now.

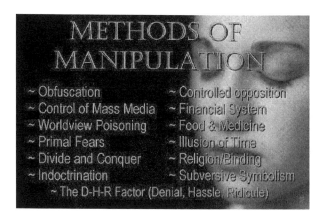

The great mind Michel Foucault considers writing about yourself to be what he terms a technology of the self. Writing is used as a tool to say and discover something about yourself in such a way that you could become different. Forms of personal and private writing bring us close to a type of knowledge that transforms us. Through personal writings about ourselves, we produce new ways of being. Through the writing, we practise a freedom to be a different self. This freedom transforms us and grants us power to pronounce truths about ourselves that may lead others to transform themselves. I write, and will continue to write, in order to reinforce new beliefs and to become different. By becoming different, I practise a transformative freedom, which I hope will lead others to find freedom and also change, be it a little or a lot. I guess you could say that I agree with Michel Foucault, a great mind, who for me has hit the nail on the head.

It is my hope that within my ramblings a person will find at least one nugget (hopefully more!) that will help give more meaning to his or her world, meaning at the level at which most of us live, on the ground, in the real world, and not with our heads in the clouds. In this book I will discuss how I try to live my philosophy from day to day. I am not entirely sure what my philosophy is, and I am changing daily. I never really succeed 100 per cent in my aims, but I am mindful of much that I had never even been aware of previously in my life. The structure will be quite random, as that is how life and thoughts arrive with me, how I reflect on them and thus develop my reflections. I have yet to learn how to think in nice, ordered chapters.

Much has been written about the flow of the universe; well, I consider that is how I write. An idea presents itself when the time is right. There follow many random thoughts and ideas for me to ingest. We will enter the random world of my daily thought processes. You may think it self-indulgent to talk about oneself in a book, but I hope the following arguments will help state my case. I can only view the world from my unique perspective; attempting anything else would be foolhardy. I wholeheartedly resist the "proper way to write" behaviours in favour of the - I write – you understand – job done scenario. I write as best I can to be understood and then readers agree or disagree. That is the whole point of writing to promote thoughts that one likes or does not like. There is far too much time wasted on critiquing style and conformist writing habits when it should be concentrated on the ideas, messages and thoughts of any communication. I will signpost as promised any worthy writing that I know will help your awareness. There is much to be read.

We all want the same thing – to know the meaning of our existence and that is the personal journey we are all on. Behind all the desires of humanity the one desire is peace of mind. Peace of mind can visit any person no matter the circumstances and is the result of inner work not the biggest pile of stuff or the most sexual partners. Peace of mind is elusive and worthy of the challenge it may take to achieve. Nothing worth having ever comes easily. Peace of mind is the hidden treasure. Or maybe perfect peace of mind would mean we search no more and that we need that drive towards greater meaning in our lives. Quite possibly the search is where the treasure is to be found.

Existentialist philosophy argues that when you ask about the meaning of life or existence, you are really asking about the nature of active, participatory existence. You want to know what the significance is of your way of existing that is different from others'. You have no way to detach from your own participation with existence, so you should approach and understand your existence through an analysis of how living itself happens or what it is like to be an active participator.

Nietzsche rejects the notion of a right way to see things. He sees no objective truth in the world to be discovered. Instead, he thinks you must understand the world through your perspective, one that always reflects your own specific interests. He thinks there are no facts, just interpretations. His view is called perspectivism, the view that all descriptions of the world are given from a biased or self-interested point of view. Furthermore, although you hold at any given moment a given perspective, you're never reducible to that perspective. Your identity is never fixed; new perspectives are always possible for you.

One of the key aims of this book is to provide all of this in an easy-to-read, easy to understand style. I have found that often (not always) academic writing can be difficult or impossible to understand. I do not consider myself an academic. Labelling and being labelled is one of my pet hates, but it's difficult to avoid. Academics' discourse gives them power over others who are not as proficient in the discourse, and so they maintain a hierarchy which keeps them in an elevated position. By using their own language, or a version of the same language, they effectively exclude many of us who might benefit from their learned message. I hope to bridge the gap, thus providing a more readable access to some of the ideas of the great thinkers, while I have a foot in both camps. Is that allowed? It's probably not encouraged, but the writer of a book based on getting better has to take the chance not to conform if the end looks to justify the means. I am sure I will get crucified from all sides. It is so easy to criticise.

> *At no point do I claim any special mastery over how to live life, but I am committed to finding a formula through experience that could assure a person some success.*

—Benjamin Franklin

I am claiming nothing with my work other than being a messenger for the many fine people out there that are wide awake and uncovering truths that we all should be aware of. I aim to give guidance on becoming aware and to share some of my thoughts on many different subjects close to us all.

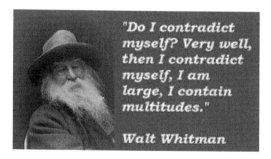

"Do I contradict myself? Very well, then I contradict myself, I am large, I contain multitudes."

Walt Whitman

This book is not a typical self-help book. My principal wish is to inspire thought, create unrest, disturb sleep and contribute some broader perspective than what is immediately on offer, waiting to be plucked ready made from the limited choice available on the society opinions shelf.

7

I will not inform you how to discover God, find the partner of your dreams or how to make friends and influence others. That is your personal calling not mine. I respect your potential to create perhaps more than you do. I know you will not avoid all of life's experiences, temptations and distractions surround you, and that fear and pressure to conform to norms weaken your soul and diminish your progress.

I believe that for you to progress you will have to become more responsible than your conformist nature wishes you to be. I acknowledge the monumental significance of spirituality in this undertaking and of claiming back your life and becoming more whole. I affirm no particular belief for you to adopt. Again, that is your calling.

This book is based on a personal and ongoing journey as I began with "Dazed and Confused' & 'More Rebel than Zen'. The progress made between the three books is marked. My writing style has been described as self-deprecating and chatty. I prefer to think I write to you as I might talk to you if we met, clearly, respectfully and passionately. I contradict myself often and at times the actual scope of our life on earth leaves my head in a spin. However, the contradiction is all part of the process of getting better for an open mind.

My aim is that my work is always challenging you to find your answers to the ongoing questions that your life asks of you. Your journey is uniquely your journey, not someone else's. It is never the wrong time to start. The best time is always now.

I wish to suggest that all books help us become more than we are when we begin to read them. I will even go as far as to state that if a book is not going to help then we should not be reading it. However, that is not likely as even the mindful behaviour of focusing on reading for a reasonable amount of time helps our minds. In the last few years I have mentored young men who could not focus even to get past the first page in any book. They lacked the attention span. A common occurrence in the 21st century.

Even the resistance to certain words contained in books holds a valuable lesson. For me the word God was guaranteed to have me stop reading any book as being too religious. Then I realised that I had learned through my conditioning, that religious people were a bit 'special' and not in a good way had blocked my learning and my ability to formulate my own thoughts, ideas and opinions. I was narrow minded when it came to religion. I had been brainwashed to believe what others wanted me to believe. I have since expanded my awareness and I have even developed my own personal concept of God and flexible world view in general, which is more an acceptance of never being able to truly know, as any God that words can describe cannot be God. Let's face it we are all pretty clueless but have an inkling and that may be all we need. More importantly I have a much more open mind and love to allow others their own thoughts also. This can be true in many areas. If resistance is experienced there is a lesson to learn. I am now willing to learn and hold no views that are so fixed that they may never change.

My point is that this book is a self-help book, as they all are. It is the aim of this book to help all readers to progress. There are many areas for getting better, so many that I feel I can't fail in my aim for all readers to progress in some way from the experience of reading this book. Even the act of disagreeing with every single point I raise is progress away from indifference or holding readymade opinions.

I aim to relate quite complex ideas in an easy to read and understand format that bridges the gap between academic work and mainstream texts.

I will use personal anecdotes to make the theories become real for you. Everything contained in this book we are living in every moment. That is an important lesson, I am writing about your life and my life. The ability for you to relate the contents of this book to yourself is vital to your progress and mine. And in fact vital to any learning process. Life is a learning process. We are learning to become whole, to unite a fragmented psyche, body and soul in a way that makes us feel better and maybe even provides some meaning to a life lacking any real meaning to this point. What that means will become about as clear as mud in this book. That is all part of the process and the moments of clarity do become more common and very welcome.

As the person choosing to read this book you are in a constant process of change. The aim of this book is to help you ensure that the changes you experience are progressive. The act of reading this book or any other such book ensures that a different you complete the reading and places the book down than the one that picked it up to begin reading in the first place. All books change your life, it is my aim that this book will have a profound effect on every reader and that your state of mind will become one of progress in each and every aspect of your existence.

If this book were to have a research question, it would be as follows:

How might we learn to master the art of awareness towards personal progression in order to create peace of mind and heart, give meaning to, and shape the direction of our lives for the benefit of our souls, the planet and mankind? In a nut shell – How can we get better?

The scope of the subject is colossal, however my aim is simple, to guide my readers, my clients and myself to a life of progression. A life full of meaning and a life to be lived to the full until we eventually and predictably arrive at the bridge into the unknown. For now, we can only live the lives we know we have. We have a finite timescale barring any abrupt endings. Life is unpredictable so we best get on with it. Nobody really knows past 'lights out' what the future holds. It would be pointless and a terrible waste of time not to live for this time whilst banking on immortality. We can live well and progress right now and if there turns out to be continued consciousness for humans past physical death then I believe that is called a win-win situation. There is no place for narrow mindedness or resistance to personal change. We have to be as receptive to change in ourselves as we seem to be to new technology. If the new technology amazes you? You are in for a rare treat once you begin to understand what you might be capable of. The authentic version of you is far more impressive than the latest model of any chosen gadget. When you begin to learn how to unite body and mind as one mindbody the mind becomes like the ultimate gadget with infinite lights and buzzers that previously have been hidden from awareness. I am learning to use my mind with my body as I believe that consciousness (mind) is the guiding factor in what we are and what we are to become. Contained within consciousness are the possibilities of what it ultimately means to be human and free. We are capable of so much more and upon this awareness human evolution may accelerate away from the controlling mechanisms designed to hold us back.

Change is inevitable. Human beings and much of life on earth are evolving and changing more rapidly than ever before. There are two useful rules for readiness and acceptance of change, keep an open mind and make the change progressive whenever there is personal choice involved. We are learning that we have more control over who we are than we ever dreamt possible. True enough, there are barricades to turn into bridges but they become bridges all too easily once the awareness, belief and expectations become great and the old myths have been exploded or more likely re-interpreted.

The hardest task is probably understanding what we are at this moment in time:

How did we become this self?

What are the forces that have determined who we are and can we break free from these forces?

Can we really become anything we want to be?

Can we become whole, sacred, enlightened, saved, a higher self, authentic or any of the other terms used to describe a human being making progress beyond the rigid and widely accepted norms?

Are you happy being the norm, the same as other norms?

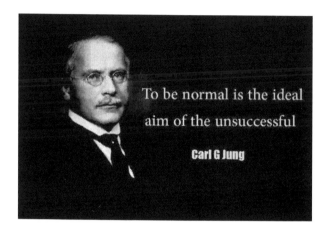

To be normal is the ideal
aim of the unsuccessful

Carl G Jung

I have possible answers for all of these questions in my life and I feel the outlook is very good. You will develop your own answers as you live your life to the full. I am not saying it will be easy. Easy is never rewarding. However, the human race has many problems caused by fragmented psyches, cultural conditioning and our selfish genes. All of these can be overcome. Now more than ever before, we are capable of transcending our nature, cultural conditioning and mastering our psyches in order to take the human race onto a new level of development. The answer to all of them is to be found inside of us. By each of us becoming all we can be, the human collective will become all that it can be. As the saying goes - if you want to change the world then start with yourself. Fairy steps will get the job done. Impatience will not. The human race is on the move and we are all involved.

This is not even taking into account the amazing possibilities being discovered within Quantum physics and the afterlife experiments. I will recommend books for you to pore over at the end and on my website www.adamsenex.com. Reading widely is both essential and an amazing voyage leading to the discovery of what may be going on behind our backs and what other humans are discovering and achieving across the globe. The changed beliefs may take a while longer to filter through the archaic and fearful resistance to change, but when it comes Human beings may become super beings compared to what we are today. 100 years is not long for so much radical change and the changes and discoveries are most definitely that. All that we become can be paid forward to future generations. The future of the human race is so finely balanced; we could become extinct in record time or accelerate into a new era. And that future either way is in our hands, mind, body and soul. Each and every one of us has a duty to leave a legacy of progressing as far as we can before we check out. Memories and behaviours last far longer than material objects. Getting better until the day we die. It couldn't be simpler. All the best ideas are simple. Even dying is a mystery tour. Nobody knows what that journey into the unknown holds in store for us but I am very well read and the knowledge and wisdom I have gained leaves me more optimistic than ever. Reading has given me a world view that is far more optimistic than I could possibly obtain from the media, science, second hand religions and acceptance of conformist views of how the world is and how it might be in our imagined futures. Although all of these inevitably contribute to our world view.

This book will provide signposts for that positive change that I will quite simply be calling progress. All we need to ensure is that we choose progress each time we get a choice, however small the choice may seem and eventually the snowball effect will change the world via memes and actual physical change to our brains. We will be happier, more understanding and tolerant of others differences and the world will become a better place.

What exactly does progress entail and in what areas can we progress?

Improved awareness - More curious - More knowledge – Better listening - Improved self-image - Better nutrition – New attention for life lessons – Loving relationships – Fitter body - Better understanding - New jobs – New opportunities – New adventures everyday – Less addictions & attachments – Less depression & anxiety – Less fear - Less anger...............Empowerment.

In short we can progress in every aspect of our lives, every day and in as yet undiscovered ways. We are experts in getting better, all we need is to just get in the spirit of progress. Once immersed we can't fail to improve our lives and touch all others that we come into contact with. A win-win situation.

There is so much progress to make. I could fill the book with areas for progress. Progress includes anything that you want it to include. Now that is a lot of choices and a life packed full of progress and motivation.

All we have to do is improve ourselves, now that isn't too much to ask. And while we reap the personal benefits of a better life we are all impacting the planet in one big progressive tidal wave.

> "Before beginning a Hunt, it is wise to ask someone what you are looking for before you begin looking for it............You can't always sit in your corner of the forest and wait for people to come to you... you have to go to them sometimes."
>
> - Pooh Bear

You have begun to look. I am here to tell you what to look for and the rest is up to you. Happy hunting.

Life is a process and our life purpose is to progress throughout the process as we live it or as forces dictate we live it. This life purpose could not be simpler but as I mentioned all of the best ideas are simple and have been inside of us all along. So look no further for your life purpose, here it is. Could our life purpose be **to progress to wholeness in the process of life, for the betterment of self, others, the planet and beyond?** Quite simply to get better every day in every way.

There is nothing difficult or demanding about any of the theories. Progressing is more about changing the way we think than learning any new talents. We are everything we need to be in our souls. We are all learners and as such we are partners in the endeavour to progress the human race, beginning with ourselves. In my life-coaching practice the term we use for all of our interactions is partnerships. We each have something to offer and are at differing stages of our progress, with differing talents and abilities but ultimately we are all one. We must not feel better or worse than one another. That is the first lesson of progress. The important thing is the message. Possibly, the most important partner in our progress is our own subconscious mind. I call my subconscious mind my soulmate. My subconscious is my soulmate in success. It can either be our greatest ally or our biggest obstacle.

 ## Learning - The Aliveness of Progress

All we can do, and all we will do is to learn what we are ready to learn. And all that takes is an absorption in learning, in observing, in contemplation and in trying to understand our own nature. This active learning is participatory, is life long and interesting, in its own way it's a blessing.

We are in the position of looking around from where we are standing, our starting point and observing those areas we do not understand and that are still unknown. There is no place for know it alls in this endeavour. We know nothing. We are all in that position and it provides access to constant freshness and the delight of discovering the new, the unseen and the yet uncontrolled, this is the aliveness of progress.

We must not fear failure, that we will make mistakes and not guess where we will find the ultimate prize. There is no prize to be found. There is only the process of becoming more balanced, more authentic, and truly alive. If we observe, we will see exactly what our eyes are able to see and use at that precise moment and if we can have some faith in that process, we will enjoy our lives and progress and be free from the fear that imprisons us where we are now.

There is nothing to fear, nothing to lose, only the adventure of learning, of release, of curiosity and awe at the expansive reality, possibilities exceeding anything we have experienced, yet to which we are invisibly attached as one.

 Allowed To Be

I am probably not alone in spending the majority of my life believing myself ordinary and unexceptional and as such with nothing of interest to say to people on how they may live their lives. Retrospectively I have always had this feeling of never really belonging in groups and a feeling of being the odd one out in most group situations. A good example would be on the odd occasion I would go to a soccer match with my friends. They would comfortably exhibit the herd behaviour seen as normal in that situation I would just feel silly and not understand the behaviour at all, finding it, for want of a better word, senseless. Thus I would end the experience feeling that there was something wrong with me in that I could not enjoy the bonding as the others so obviously were. In fact, I think the herd had the opposite effect on me and rather than provide a place to hide away or to be comfortable and avoid personal responsibilities, the experience actually made me feel more separate and I felt that all others could see I did not belong and were aware of my discomfort. Rather than hide in the crowd I felt exposed and vulnerable in the crowd. I do now wander just how many of them were authentically in the moment and how many were being inauthentic and just playing their expected roles as football supporter things. Struggling just as I was at that time with the need to belong to something even if it means masking who we really are in our hearts for fear of rejection.

IF YOU'RE YOUR *authentic self*, YOU HAVE NO COMPETITION.

However, over time and more comfortable as my fake self I have learned how to adapt rather than become comfortable and can "fit in" with the required herd mentality when needed albeit begrudgingly at times, even more so in recent times.

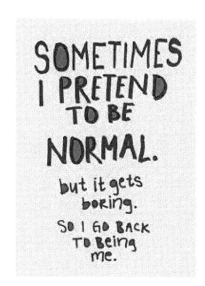

SOMETIMES I PRETEND TO BE NORMAL. but it gets boring. So I go back to being me.

More recently, within the last decade or so, my attitude has changed from one of a kind of apologetic inability to tailor myself to each and every group situation, to an attitude of understanding that it is ok to be just how I am and my freedom is to be found in that, and other choices that previously I had felt separated me from society in a negative way. I think the best way to explain myself is that up to the point that I consider my awakening moment **my life lived me.**

I was sleepwalking through a life that was based on others, norms and societies expectations. I had little awareness of the situation and believed myself to be freely living my own life. However, the nagging doubts and anxieties were ever present and I forever tried to find peace of mind in more is better. More stuff, more fun, just more distractions in general but those "something missing" moments never really left me. Material gains and hedonistic pleasure were my unfulfilling answers and the short term solutions to my problems. I see now that that is the case for many "normal" members of our society and they are lost in the more is better philosophy in the search for that promised happiness that they believe they deserve and is possible because it has been promised, and is falsely promised every day in many different ways through the gadgets we can no longer live without. They are the wrong answers. They will never be the right answers. That next new car, holiday, gadget, relationship or night out will do very little but postpone the search for that deeper meaning that we all crave in reality but are for too distracted to ever give any real thought or effort to obtaining.

I now live my life as opposed to being carried along by norms and opinions. I dare to be myself and aim for authenticity as much as I can. I am also aware that 100% authenticity may or may not be attainable as we are conditioned from birth to behave inauthentically. For the first time in my life I feel I am seeing life and particularly life for an individual in society clearly, or more clearly. The challenge and meaning that brings to my life is invigorating and inspires me to enjoy every moment with a renewed vigour. This renewed vigour or passion is not to be seen and exhibited by external actions but a deeper internal feeling, a passion for life and a life full of eureka moments that make you smile inwardly. For the first time in my life a comfortable feeling of having an understanding of what I can and can't expect from my life. A feeling of knowing that the meaning of my life is entirely down to my choices. A feeling of understanding that man will never have all of the answers that he so desires and that that desire for clarity is often misplaced, so misplaced that he would rather invent answers and lies than accept that life is absurd and the clarity pursued by man is unattainable. And lastly a realisation that there are no absolute systems, not science, religion or rational thought that will ever provide the answers for each and every individual on this planet despite their rather extravagant claims of having all of the answers we will ever need. If they do not have the answer, then the problem does not exist. It is up to each individual to create the meaning to their lives and to take responsibility. You have more choices than you realise and there are never any guarantees that you will make the right choice or that when a choice doesn't work out that the other choice would have worked out any better.

Choose and move on. The way forward is through awareness of what is and was is not and can never be. And an awareness that you as an individual are pure possibilities and you are constantly becoming, constantly renewing yourself till the day you eventually become a fixed entity, the day you expire. At that moment you will enter the transition we call death, one of the biggest mysteries and you will be able to discover first hand if your personal answer to that big question is accurate. That is providing you have thought for yourself enough to have a personal view as opposed to the wholesale opinions that are available off the peg from our myriad of religions. Maybe you could explore all of them and find your own comfort zone in amongst the confused dogma.

THE FIRST STEP TOWARD CHANGE IS AWARENESS. THE SECOND STEP IS ACCEPTANCE.

NATHANIEL BRANDEN

QuotePixel.com

This book is designed to help the reader progress by breaking free of at least some of the society conditioning and automaton thoughts that pervade any culture. Thoughts that are aimed at social control, security and profit for the ruling classes rather than for the good of the individual. I am thinking and attempting to live this philosophy oftentimes against the society grain each and every day. Your whole life may change and the people in it also as you no longer play your old roles to fit in. Sometimes I manage to live free and authentically and at other times I get dragged back into the comfort of herd mentality and inauthenticity. The project never ends and the aim is to live a truly free individual life in a society that will assimilate you totally back into the collective with its considered normal and expected beliefs and behaviours if you choose to surrender your freedom. That is the fate that awaits if I relax even for one second. What a buzz that passion creates inside, what a challenge, every day a life to be lived by me or given away to relative comfort and conformity (enslavement).

> "In every encounter with reality man is already beyond this encounter. He knows about it, he compares it, he is tempted by other possibilities, he anticipates the future as he remembers the past. This is his freedom, and in this freedom the power of his life consists. It is the source of his vitality, of his life power". - Paul Tillich

I am getting better and that is the best I can expect, maybe that is the best we can all expect. Having said that I have never found life more interesting than I do now and having the life purpose of transcending myself every day is certainly a purpose worthy of my life. A life with meaning and a purpose that anybody can adopt. There are ups and downs but an acceptance of the downs as all part of the process does make them an interesting proposition and often the best lessons are contained in the downs.

I write about awareness, progress, getting better and how that might work for us all in the real world. My writing by necessity is probably more rebel than Zen due to the numerous discoveries by other authors of what might be happening behind our backs. I attempt to map personal progress despite all of our obstacles. I consider myself a messenger for many fine writers and an interpreter of complicated ideas into an understandable and practical language.

With the **Getting Better series of books** I write to motivate, inspire and teach optimism in a very difficult world. I cover all aspects of life from health and fitness, work, relationships and everything in between to the best of my ability at the stage I am at in that precise moment in my life. Getting better in the real world – whatever that might mean!

We would all like to be perfectly Zen a calm amongst the turbulent world and that was my initial intention with my writing. 100% constructive, positive and optimistic throughout it all but it soon became blatantly clear that there is much going on behind our backs and that approach would be unrealistic and quite frankly unworkable in a world that has many demons and not enough heroes and angels. If we wish to get better, we can't begin by ignoring anything that may make us uncomfortable. There is much in human society that will make us very uncomfortable indeed. I will signpost books to read for you to understand more fully to what I may be referring. But you will need a very open mind and to understand that much of what you think you know now is programming. Your learning and world view will be unique to you and will be a process of constant change and discovery.

What do we do with all of this awareness, how can we help?

We simply work to get better ourselves, we don't waste energy on resisting the rest of the world that we are unhappy about. We raise ourselves above it all.

The all important thing is to live our lives at the highest possible energy level that we can attain and the more of us that are able to do this the better the world will be. It really is that simple.

Everything changes when you start to emit your own frequency rather than absorbing the frequencies around you, when you start imprinting your intent on the universe rather than receiving an imprint from existence.

~ Barbara Marciniak ~

OkyDay.com

There is a battle on this planet between higher and lower energy and much of what we see on the news would indicate that lower energy has control of this planet. That is our task, to change the energy of the planet, to take it so high that the lower energy just fades out of awareness completely. You have heard the saying "ignore them and they will go away". By ignoring them we are not using our energy to boost them. We must not get dragged down to their level, we created this by letting them drag us down, we can end it by taking their powers away. Their power comes from our fear and anxiety, our anger and stress is their energy source. We are being held back.

We start with ourselves and support our friends and loved ones if they are on the same journey and that is how we save this planet and evolve the human race. We do it by recognising that our hearts and minds create our worlds and everything else is just a distraction and an effort to stop humanity reaching its full potential. Or as many would say the dark side of the human mind prevailing over the light.

Probably the best thing we can do, is to approach it all with a sense of humour and not take it all so seriously and that way our state of mind will be perfect and ever so slightly annoying to those that want us to live in fear.

Responsibility

With awareness comes great change, there may come a feeling of being chosen particularly if a landmark moment of suffering or similar has led us to this awareness. We may feel set apart and our thoughts and ideas may actually set us apart from the world we knew before this moment, it may be a gradual and slow awakening or it could be a sudden epiphany that can be traced to the very second the change began. The process of coming to the realisation that you no longer fit your world quite so well can be gradual but it will happen. This can manifest in anyone of us who has found our individual path or is just finding a different path to the one we were on. "You've changed" is what we hear and it will be accurate and we will feel estranged from those that have not changed and that may well be most of the people that we knew well to this point. This is simply what I have witnessed and experienced myself. At first we may pretend to be normal but once the hunger for awareness begins there is no going back, our world view has changed and will continue to change as long as we seek our own personal truth. We

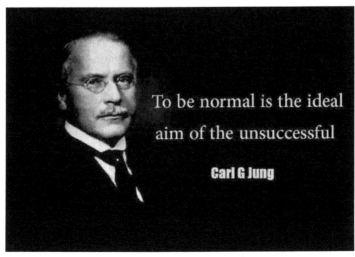

To be normal is the ideal aim of the unsuccessful

Carl G Jung

then may try to preach and open the eyes of our significant others but that is also foolhardy as awareness seems to be something that just happens like a fruit ripening. For some it may never happen.

Those of us who have begun and continue to work on ourselves are fluid and within a process and we don't care to spend much time pretending to be normal with other normal people. We try only to find that even the shortest period of time being agreeable and listening to old friends can exhaust our psychic energy. Wondering if and how we ever felt the same way as them. The differences in thoughts and behaviours increase and the ever expanding worldview of an aware individual does not compare with a conformist worldview.

This could be viewed as elitist and I for one used to feel terribly guilty and isolated due to these differences and the fact that I could no longer be who I was expected to be. I am still struggling to come to terms with the changes now. I have suffered some big losses and very few gains when it comes to flesh and blood additions to my intimate world. We are in the minority and considered a bit weird and also we test others certainties about everything in their worlds and that does not sit well unless it is self-discovered and evolves naturally. I am sure that is how I would have felt pre-awareness also. Oddly enough I do find more people that I come across casually in passing are more likely to be awakened. It's as if I have a sign on me saying "it's safe to be yourself around me, I won't think you are crazy". Julie is amazed at how I seem to draw unique individuals to me and how they open up very quickly but I guess I am like that to. As for being elitist? It is only natural not to spend time with people that you no longer have much in common with. It is after all, me that has changed. I had heard people comment that "they have gone a bit weird or strange" for others that have become estranged from their social group. I guess that is me now. I no longer fit the entry requirements and I understand totally. My life has now been changing for a decade and is unrecognisable from my previous life. Much less fake and not having to be something for others. However, that is still a work in progress. Other people have a huge effect on our personalities and lives. Jean Paul Sartre called it being-for-others. I don't spend so much of my time being-for-others as I used to and is the norm for society. I believe the norms are changing, as they must as more of us strive to find ourselves.

With awareness and a sense of purpose comes the realisation that our time on earth is precious. We become reluctant to squander it on explaining ourselves to those who don't know who they are or why they are here and are not even curious, believing that they have all of the answers already. Gained from the mainstream media and conditioned into us from birth. However, that does not make us saints or gurus but merely sets us on a different path to understanding and interested in different aspects of life previously unexplored for us. Our worlds from the inside out, always with curiosity and minds wide open. It does mean we reject, question or just plain ignore for a quite life all conformist beliefs held by the majority of others. Becoming aware can be lonely but I am sure there are more aware people ready to question conformist beliefs than there was a decade ago and that means awareness will continue to be less lonely as the years pass and the seeds having been sown begin to reap the truth. I am lucky to be sharing my journey with Julie at this point in my life. We are spiritual partners although we are progressing differently. The support for our "funny little ways" and very different (not normal) attitudes is a Godsend.

Previous to this awareness we are, to a greater or lesser extent imprisoned in society and devoted to our jail. This happens because we live in a culture that has lost objectivity, we are too influenced by our conditioning, until awareness enters our lives we can't see past the assumptions and beliefs we are immersed in, and indoctrinated into, since birth and there is some evidence to show that this begins in the womb. This is understandable even though it remains one's personal responsibility to overcome such brainwashing at some point in our lives. There is a pressing need to become curious and to evaluate more critically what is being said throughout our lives.

Because conformism has reached the position of mainstream worldview, conformists seem confident in feeling that they don't need to properly understand what they are criticising before they

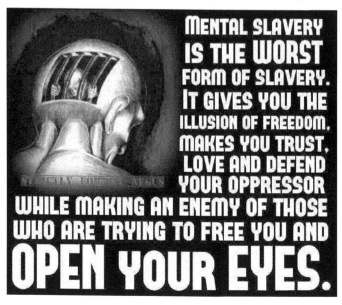

act. They are little more than ignorant representatives of mainstream conformist thought. Protected by the power and dominance afforded by the majority, some don't even seem to feel they need to think straight. But this is hardly surprising when it is not their original thought in the first place. There is very little original thought needed when assuming the same views as the majority of others handed down from on high.

 Start Where You Are

One of the most important aspects of improving oneself and personal progress and development is knowing where you are starting from. Who am I and how did I develop this personality? Human beings seem to live their lives in two parts, often named as the first half of life and the second half of life. This can be mis-leading as the parts are hardly ever exactly half of life. The second half of life being a kind of awakening from an unconscious, conditioned slumber that we are all exposed to in the first half of life. Awareness is a blessing. Some may never awaken to the second half of life while others awaken quite early as they may never have completely conformed to the early life conditioning with which they are bombarded constantly to create docile citizens, all the better for social control. They have felt misplaced as if they don't belong. They have felt different and uncomfortable. Mostly introverts attempting to survive in an extravert's 'first half of life' culture. They live with an underlying unrest. Knowing there must be more to life for them. They are right. They come into their own in the second half of life as if this moment is what they have been waiting for all of their lives. The awakening can be as early as the twenties or for some, never. Many preferring the comfort of conformist society. How do we become who we are to this point?

From birth, maybe before, our personas (masks or false selves) begin to develop according to our societies, significant others, rules, regulations and customs. We observe behaviour and decide what is to be part of our act and what is to be dismissed from our acceptable persona. At exactly the same time as we chose our personas, running parallel to our persona development is the development of our personal shadow. This part of our psyches contains all of the qualities that don't fit our self-image or the image expected of us by numerous others. If we are expected to be polite, then rudeness and bad manners will be buried deep in our shadows. It is the place where our darker sides live and at the same time much of our stifled creativity and positive stuff that is just not approved of by our cultures up to now. If we are raised to be intolerant of difference, then our tolerance of difference will be in our shadow. You are getting the picture by now. A tough, violent gang member will have love and compassion in his shadow. A hardnosed business man possibly the same lest anybody gets all self-righteous, we all have shadow sides that contain much we wouldn't like to broadcast but a healthy psyche does need to accept that side and balance persona and shadow for a healthy mature psyche.

Persona and shadow develop in tandem, creating each out of the one life experience. Add to this the presence of the sacred authentic self, often termed the watcher and we have quite a busy psyche for one person to balance and align. Many factors contribute to forming both the persona and our shadow selves, deciding what is permitted for us and what is not. Parents, siblings, teachers, clergy, friends and even the media create a complex world where hopefully we learn what is kind, correct and accepted behaviour and what is spiteful, shameful and sinful. As mentioned good traits can be assigned to the shadow when for instance it is not considered cool to be kind or caring. In the world of some 'real men' being kind and caring would be considered a weakness. The shadow need not be all darkness and gloom but is constructed from values surplus to requirement. So it is to be expected and accepted that it will contain many dark thoughts that will surprise and astound you once you begin to notice them surfacing. We are all things.

The shadow is widely thought to contain all of our undeveloped talents and gifts. When deciding what is acceptable to persona and what is to be buried it is worth noting that the seven deadly sins, namely pride, envy, greed, lust, gluttony, anger and sloth can all be observed as normal behaviour by many developing human beings. All, except sloth maybe, seem to be essential, or at least a potential asset to a successful capitalist society. Capitalism would not prosper without greed. I would go as far as to suggest that many developing young human beings receive a lifetime masterclass in all of the above 'sins'. Would this indicate that the opposite worthy traits are buried deep in their personal shadows awaiting exposure to the light of day for the very first time? Traits such as humility and generosity never being part of the personas shown to the world.

I deal with how we form our personas in much greater detail in the upcoming section – a must read for any aspiring seeker. Knowing what is, or may be happening behind your back is crucial to progressing. Forewarned is forearmed.

 Who and how are we now?

Before taking on the task of revealing our true selves it will serve us well to discover how we became who we are right now. There are many theories as to how we construct our identities or maybe more to the point how we are conditioned to be a certain way by society norms and learned behaviours. It can seem as though we pick our identities from a selection to suit any given situation. We often have many different identities selected to enable us to fit in. For example, a man may have the role of Father, son, husband, work colleague, team mate and political candidate. All these roles needing a different self in order to adapt to each role successfully. Success in any role is measured by society standards (norms) and judged mainly by one's peers and public opinion. Adopting behaviour other than the norm (non-conformism) can lead to disapproval and even the chance of being ostracized. Even behaviours that eventually become the norm can at first be the cause of an uncomfortable life for the pioneering society member daring to introduce behaviour against the current conditioning. As an example – there are many house husbands today but the original concept left the pioneering men open to ridicule and accusations of laziness due to the existing inherited beliefs that a real man has to provide for the poor weak woman. There are still remnants of these beliefs today and it normally takes many generations for the new behaviour to become as dogmatic as the original belief. The original couples that reversed the expected roles were brave and would have suffered much abuse from friends and family for their lifestyle choice. However, the seed was sowed in people's minds that there are more choices available than the conformist choice, thus opening up a new thought process and offering new choices to many. From this it becomes obvious that whilst we are free to construct our identities there are unseen and ever changing power relations limiting just who we are now and who we can become in the future. All such dogmatic conformist beliefs are open to change for the open minded and curious souls amongst us. The change may be less comfortable than conformism but it is living rather than behaving as an automaton like all the other automatons.

One point amongst others that I hope to make with this book is that there lies at our core an authentic self that is not part of this creative process and that rather than create a self the ultimate purpose for us all is to strip away the layers of fake identity to reveal and maintain the perfection that is our true selves. The best way I have heard this transformation described is that - our purpose in life is to align our ego personalities with our shadows, becoming whole, thus revealing our sacred selves, I call this quite simply getting better. I feel this inner work is best approached gently but with purpose.

Let us now look at some of the ways we have created the identities that we can now begin to work at stripping away and dispense with to reveal who we really are.

Ego - Personality – Concepts Of The Self

When the aim is to reduce the ego it may be helpful to know a little more about it. Following is my take on various concepts of the self (ego) from academic and spiritual sources. This may offer a more complete picture of how and why the ego develops and allow a better understanding of how it may be reduced if indeed the personal feeling is that It must be reduced. All of these concepts are contributing factors towards developing one's identity. All of these are developed unconsciously as part of social conditioning and relationships with others. We rarely question who we are until the ego has developed in such a way that we are led to question who we are. Identity is never a conscious forming of a self. Awareness comes upon reflection when knowing yourself may reveal what has been going on behind your back from birth. It can be very sobering to wake up one day and realize that you have been virtually unconscious until that point in your life. All behaviours, opinions and reactions have been automatic. Programmed into you since birth and reinforced on a daily basis. To realize that your freedom has been an illusion along with most of your ego driven existence. To realize that the self that you thought was you is just an impostor and the real you is watching the impostor. Becoming aware begins the journey home to your sacred self. Once the ego is revealed it can no longer hide and disguise itself well enough to fool you like it has been for the early part of your life. The feeling is as if there has been a separate entity running your life without your full permission or permission at all. You may actually feel quite angry at the fact that you have had less choice than you realized in becoming who you thought you were. The biggest thought for me was the awareness that I didn't know who I was at all. I had become whatever forces outside of myself had wanted me to become, or at least I had been limited to growth within the boundaries that those invisible forces deemed acceptable. Mostly for social control which includes ensuring profit for the ruling classes as they get richer and at the same time the masses consume and stay exactly where they are for the reward of an ever growing pile of stuff and gadgets. Accumulating stuff distracts people from ever asking, is there more to life? And if the question crosses your mind and an answer is not readily available on the meaning of your existence in a second or less then the search is too much trouble and becomes buried beneath whatever activity prevents you from having to deal with the serious questions that will out at some time. However, this is not about starting a revolution it is about awareness and living one's life on purpose. And let me tell you that feels very good. The awareness brings with it a purpose for one's life and gives meaning to an increasingly mundane existence. To do that it helps to know what goes on, or may be going on behind one's back.

I like to view all humans as being somewhere along a continuum. At one end we would find enlightened beings with no real self at all of which there are very few and at the other end we may find totally soul-less beings maybe such as mass murderers or the perpetrators of some of the most heinous crimes known to man. Lots or all soul at one end and no soul at the other end. I firmly believe we all fall somewhere along this continuum. Preferably towards the top but maybe not so high as to have lost our essential human traits entirely. I think we are special just mis-guided for profit and social control by unseen powers. I also believe that the ego can be tamed and aligned with our shadow sides and our souls and we can be a human like never before seen. A super-human. We begin totally pure and innocent with any karmic debt added and then through conditioning and our experiences we all begin to bury and forget who we really are, our souls and what it really means to be human. That is the way things continue unless we have an epiphany, see the light, awaken or any of the other terms used for finally discovering that maybe we have been lied to all along and controlled for profit and convenience and that our real purpose is to learn our lessons and reconnect to our soul and at the same time all that there is. Alternatively, it may become a trend to start the process of being an individual and the planet will be saved by becoming authentically human being the fashionable way to be, a trend. Most of us are a complex cocktail of constructed ego personalities, repressed shadow sides and an authentic soul or pure being at the core, what Jung called the Self. Mostly operating as separate entities. The way forward? A fusion of all the opposites, such as the feminine and masculine, pride and humility and good and bad all in one psyche. The mission for us all is to align our personalities and shadows with our soul. We are as we are now in the first part of life due to the egos survival instincts, social conditioning and pure acceptance that this is the only way to be. This normally takes the form of spending much of life constructing complex selves in order, we feel, to survive and upon awakening and the realization that they are not needed. Then begins the journey home, of stripping away layer after layer of unnecessary personality and society conditioning to reveal the soul. Many humans never begin the journey home and live their lives in what can only be described as a deep sleep or unconscious of their total lack of any real freedom and choice. To most, who they believe they are is real and permanent. This is the destiny of the conformist. The vast majority of the human race. You are already past that stage just by reading to this point.

Popular thought now believes that humans are getting both better and worse. Many finding the route to their souls and many oblivious that there is even a responsibility to get better throughout life. The belief is that the future of the planet rests on the total consciousness of mankind. This balances one against the other in a ratio favouring high energy (the soul-self). The future of the planet depends on this.

This book is about getting better, physically and mentally making the most of our precious gifts. Each of us working to improve our individual consciousness to raise the planet's consciousness. Each of us is very important. If you want to improve the world, start with yourself. Even if we never actually become enlightened beings, what fun to strive for that worthy goal and to know that just by getting better we will make the universe a better place and ourselves happier. But make no mistake endless happiness is not the aim of getting better. Living a full authentic life is. A process of constant change and progression as opposed to sticking where one is now, a living death or regression.

In line with the thinking in this book at the core of genuine Buddhist teachings is the knowing that your mind causes you to suffer by superimposing permanence and constructing a separate self where, in fact, neither exists. The path to enlightenment is to reveal your true self and accept the impermanence of life. Ultimately the true self, Holy Spirit, soul or whatever other term may be used and for which we all search is in reality no self. The letting go of the need for a self is thought to lead to enlightenment and the necessary break in the birth, death and re-birth cycle.

Let's look at some relevant identity topics now and begin to learn how we become who we think we are. How we create our identities in order to survive and at the same time bury our souls deep under layers of what can only be called innocent deceit. In the next section I will briefly discuss some of the ways we form our identities and the survival identities we create.

Since feeling a sense of "I" is crucial to our sanity we are impelled to do more or less anything to possess this sense. Behind the extreme passion for status and conformity is this very drive, and it is at times stronger than the need for survival. People are willing to surrender their own thoughts, freedom, loves and risk their lives for the sake of belonging to the herd, of conforming and acquiring a sense of identity, even though it is an illusory one.

The point of this look at identity construction is to increase awareness of our role in it and following awareness there comes acceptance and then getting better by discarding the layers of unwanted identity to reveal the perfection or more realistically the authenticity at the core.

I will say that working on this book has been a revelation in how I now know myself with some very sobering insights. Each day seemed to unearth a new Adam, one that operates very much in accordance with these first sections on identity construction. But as they say knowledge is power and the awareness introduced to me has led to my life purpose of getting better becoming yet more interesting and challenging. An open mind and the knowledge that you can choose to change anything about yourself are your most valuable assets. The fact that you are the perfect fit in the perfect universe does help a little also. I will begin with looking at a number of theories of the self as this will help to understand the subsequent sections. Second I will discuss the human shadow before moving on to narcissistic personality disorder (NPD). Everything can get better.

 Identity Theories

The self, or our identity if you prefer is not fixed but is actively constructed. We are all capable of assimilating and reshaping knowledge that influences our sense of personal identity. Our identities are opened up to the domains of choice, individuality, aesthetics, disposable income and consumption. This has occurred through the mass marketing of lifestyles through advertising. Some would argue that society is so saturated with consumerist signs, codes and messages that our identities are now fully governed by dominant social interests and conditioned in advance. Continuing the argument that traditional forms of social integration have broken down leaving the self to be shaped by global capitalism and media saturation. This is either seen as an end to authenticity and freedom for human beings to be replaced by heavily conditioned automatons or an inevitable rebirth of new personal identities. As with any transformation time will tell as to whether the changes benefit or condemn the human race. There follows, some popular theories showing how this might be occurring. Some may resonate with you personally more than others but as with many theories they all may have an element of truth in them. I believe that to be true, although I do favour certain theories over others. Together they paint a very convincing picture of the idea that we are shaped by many forces outside of ourselves and maybe the way home is to look inside of our psyches where our perfection has been hidden all along.

YOU KEEP IT ON THE INSIDE 'CAUSE THAT'S THE SAFEST PLACE TO HIDE.

Symbolic Interactionism

This theory places great significance upon the social self; each of us, as individuals styles a sense of who we are through involvement with others. We exist and experience life only in as much as others exist and participate in our experience. There is a consistency to being a self and by looking at our own experiences, thoughts, feelings and attitudes through participation we can understand the actions of others. This theory could be considered deterministic in that we have no choice as to who we are and are just reflections of general society attitudes and social structures. Put bluntly, the automatons I mentioned earlier. However, the theory splits the self into 'me' and 'I'. The 'me' is the socialised, conformist self and the 'I' the unique, non-conformist part within that is more of an original thinker. Self-awareness is when the individual is able to differentiate the 'me from the 'I'. This is often called the awakening in contemporary literature. Transformation and change happens in the social structure when the 'I' finally shows up in the interactions and the lifelong process of personality development continues until death. Social interactionists claim that the use of language permits us to become self-conscious agents, reproducing the values and morality of society through our evolving capacity for self-awareness and self-understanding. There is no room in this theory for the unconscious or the idea that society might harm or damage the individual in order to gain power and social control. Both will be covered in the coming text.

Uncovering the Self

 The Self - A Theatrical Performance

Erving Goffman (1922-82) looks at the production of the self as a presentation of different roles, likening it to a stage production. He shows how individuals' stage manage impressions in different social settings. Performing the role that suits the occasion or that creates the impression that they wish to give to others. At the same time being the audience for others. Jean Paul Sartre coined the term being for others, intimating that when others are present you are "being" due to their presence. Whether you are being watched or merely aware others are present, your behaviour becomes different than if you were, or believed you were, totally alone. This would also alter depending on how familiar you are with the others present. The body in the way it moves and the way it appears is also part of the performance and there are accepted norms and ideals that are expected to be met for players to fulfil their roles adequately. Makeup, costumes and props have significant parts to play in everyday interaction as they do in the theatre. In fact, the popular media via television, film and music video calls the shots when it comes to how you should look, what you should wear and what stuff you should own to be powerful in the real world. Rarely is there any room for original thinkers in the plot. Conform or perish seems to be the golden rule. If a celebrity has the look then it is ok to copy. Goffman even describes front stage and back stage persona (ego) as being very different. The more relaxed role being the back stage role. Nevertheless, still a role. I suppose that is why sleazy magazines are able to picture celebs "off stage" and sell the amazing pictures as they are rarely if ever seen not performing for others and the cameras. Well the real news flash is that we are all doing it but nobody cares for the vast majority of us. Our performances are for smaller audiences. This is also why conspicuous consumption is so common. The phenomena of labels and branded shopping for others to see how affluent and cool you really are. Maybe that is why so many aspire to celebrity status. If one is performing each day one might as well perform for the world and reap all the perceived happiness that the adulation and material rewards will bring. I have used the word persona. Persona are the masks worn by characters in Greek tragedies. To be a person is to be a mask, to play a role. These roles are how we know ourselves and how others know us. For me, for many years the sport of bodybuilding allowed me to hide behind a suit of armour. Even though underneath it all I was still an insecure person looking for a permanent answer to the constant insecurity that we as humans all suffer from.

The real question with regards to presenting a self is - asked in two different ways

Do our roles make us the true person or mask our true self?

Is there a true self buried beneath the ego-personality or is the ego-personality all that there is?

"With any part you play, there is a certain amount of yourself in it. There has to be, otherwise it's just not acting. It's lying."

Goffman believes it is the former. To be a person, is to perform being a person. We will discover as we move on that this is not the belief of all and many including myself believe we have a true self, soul, higher self, God inside or any of the other labels used to describe our sacred selves, a true nature buried deep beneath the constructed ego. Often called the soul. Goffman's theory attributes more agency to individuals through the realisation of skilled social performance. Arguing that the individual must continually demonstrate mastery of self to others and to the social world. Goffman's theory tends to concentrate on the preservation and manipulation of the self to fit the situation. All very fake. Goffman's image of the self as a situated performer throws into doubt the emphasis on a true self which is conspicuous in many forms of social thought. The discovery of which, being what this book is based upon. The progression towards revealing our sacred-selves

"If I knew the meaning of life, would I be sitting in a cave in my underpants?"

The Reflexive Self

The reflexive self theory takes the stand that the information about the self is not happening unbeknown to the individual but rather the individual is aware and reflects on their position and status in society. That the individual is aware of what goes on to shape their identity. The theory maintains that social practices are constantly examined and changed dependant on the information being processed about those practices, this alters character accordingly. Individuals transform by reflecting and reforming. This runs counter to such theories as governmentality theories that have the individual as a victim of subtle power and social control behind their backs. It could be argued that there are reflexive individuals in society that are what is termed awake in spiritual circles but it would be very much doubted that it was the norm and most of society is oblivious to what goes on behind their backs. For example, a very low percentage of society actually read serious nonfiction books or have access to the information that is vital to worthy reflection of the serious issues in life. Instead accepting what is handed to them in the mainstream media as their own opinions or thoughts. World news reports are in all probability more fiction than fact. The internet may offer more hope for change but it does make people lazy and see life in short incomplete sound bites and quotes. And I would guess that the internet is just as controlled as the mainstream news and maybe is equally untrustworthy as a source of truth and meaning. The answers may be found in taking stock of every available source available and viewing it through more curious and doubting eyes. One has to scratch beneath the surface to be truly reflexive about any issue. The real treasure has to be mined and more often than not many books read to unearth the precious nuggets. One book leading on to others as the trail grows throughout life. Intuition the vital ingredient.

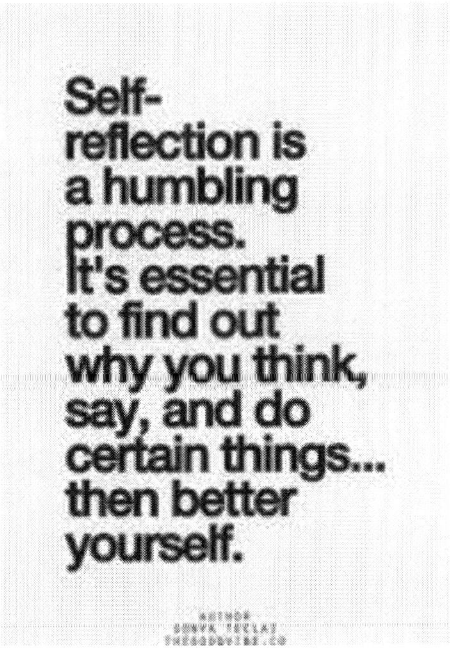

Self-
reflection is
a humbling
process.
It's essential
to find out
why you think,
say, and do
certain things...
then better
yourself.

AUTHOR
SONYA TECLAI
THEGODDVIBE.CO

Nobody plotting your course. Always the captain of your own reflexive ship. Does that sound like the norm in the 21st century? Only until a funny video comes up on the web or some other distraction halts the reflection process. Being entertained, seems to be valued above personal progress and growth. Needless to say I do not go for this theory at all. Although I do believe this to be the ideal scenario, a world where we are all awake and more intuitively aware of what is going on behind our backs and searching for answers to progress our lives towards meaning away from the party lines and conformist views. A very small minority may reflect and adjust which is what this book is about but generally it is my belief that the majority are oblivious to all I have so far written as the normal behaviour. The truths are just not available unless one reads or searches for the truth diligently over many years and with a very open mind. A lifetime process of serious reflection is what we are discussing. There are just too many distractions for the layperson to ever get past in the search for the truth they seek. There is no one truth for all of us. The truth is hidden and takes a supreme effort to find. It is hidden in plain sight though. All of the answers ever needed are inside of the individual. The last place any person would look. The books, situations, dreams and life lessons are the signposts, our map to the treasure, the revealing of the truth for each of us. Truth for each of us often turns up in the most unlikely places, all we have to do is have the courage and drive to leave the well-worn path and dare to create our own path.

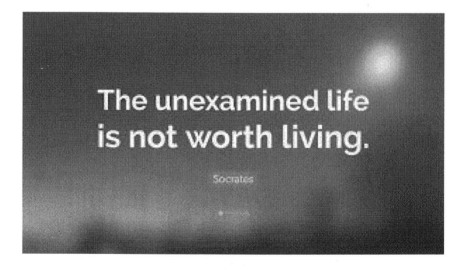

The unexamined life is not worth living.

Socrates

Next I will move onto some psychological viewpoints on how personality is constructed. I know that many of you may not want to read this section but it does help to get an idea of how we are shaped into the personality we see in the mirror and this awareness does help us to change. I have kept this section as straight forward as possible. Please give it a go. You will be pleasantly surprised.

We can change and the more we understand about ourselves the easier it is to accept and change if we wish.

Sigmund Freud

Freud opens up the realisation that our memory or our version of our own past holds clues to how we behave and who we have become. It is not simply a record of events laid out for analysis. We each have a unique way of perceiving and processing our histories.

Freud suggests that all behaviour is linked together, that are no psychological accidents – people, places, foods and amusement choices arise from experiences we do not or will not remember. All behaviours have meaning and are the result of repressed memories and emotions from our childhood development stages.

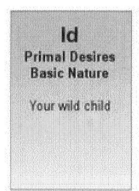

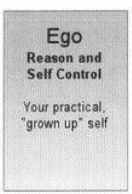

Id	Ego	Superego
Primal Desires Basic Nature	**Reason and Self Control**	**The Quest for Perfection**
Your wild child	Your practical, "grown up" self	Your philosophical and spiritual ideals

For Freud our primal impulses (id) and cultural conditioning (super ego) shape our personalities (ego). And furthermore it is the repressed and ignored material that has created our personalities and shaped our behaviour. We are of course oblivious to these forces that control our personalities. Freud, who originally began

STRUCTURAL MODEL OF PERSONALITY

According to Freud the mind can be divided into two main parts:

- **THE CONSCIOUS MIND** includes everything that we are aware of. This is the aspect of our mental processing that we can think and talk about rationally.

- **THE UNCONSCIOUS MIND** is a reservoir of feelings, thoughts, urges, and memories that outside of our conscious awareness. Most of the contents of the unconscious are unacceptable or unpleasant, such as feelings of pain, anxiety, or conflict.

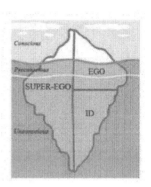

exploring the sub-conscious through hypnosis was the man that first highlighted the sub-conscious as being accessible and able to be manipulated via dreams and analysis techniques for better mental health. Freud placed great emphasis on our dreams being communications from our unconscious minds. This has been accepted and explored by others to come.

Basic principles

1. The body is the sole source of all consciousness. As opposed to there being consciousness outside of us such as Jung's collective unconscious theory.
2. Nothing occurs randomly – least of all, the individual's mental processes. All thoughts and all behaviours have meaning.

3. One's personality structure is composed of the id (it – primal urges), the ego (I – personas) and the superego (above I – society and others). The overarching goal of the psyche is to maintain an acceptable level of equilibrium that maximises the pleasure felt as tension reduction. If it hurts or is taboo we bury it deep.

4. The primary goal of psychoanalysis is to strengthen the ego, to make it independent of the overly strict concerns of the superego, and to increase its capacity to deal with material formerly repressed or hidden.

5. Dreams are used in psychoanalysis as an aid to recover unconscious material. Neither random nor accidental, dreams are considered to be one way to satisfy unfulfilled wishes. The wet dream springs immediately to mind. Happy days.

6. Early childhood experiences greatly influence teenage, young adult and adult patterns of interacting and relating. Relationships that occur in the family are the defining ones throughout an individual's later life. So Freud would always look to childhood to improve mental health. It would seem we are all screwed up by our parents and we in turn screw up our kids. Mostly done with the best of intentions.

7. We are not primarily rational animals as we would like to believe. Rather, we are often unconsciously driven by powerful emotional forces that may provide avenues for the release of tension and the appreciation of pleasure, and at the same time keep certain memories out of awareness. How often do we act in ways that surprise us and we wonder where the reaction comes from, frightening in its intensity?

Freud's View of the Human Mind:
The Mental Iceberg

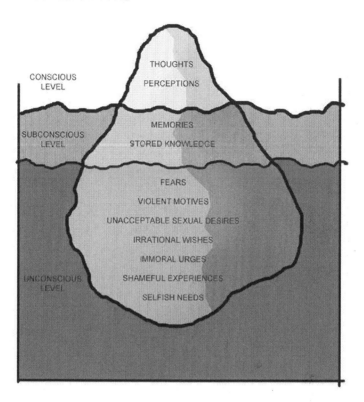

8. Given the conflicts arising from the external environment, the superego (others and society), and the relentless instinctual demands of the id (primal urges), the aim of therapy is to help establish the best possible level of ego functioning. There is a considered norm for mental health that is connected to functioning in society. It has been questioned as to whether it is best for mental health. The norm has been called insane by Fromm. And the neurotics are the types that are sensitive to this unnatural insane

norm. Is society sane? There are millions of dead humans, killed by other humans that might think not.

9. The therapist's role is to help the patient recall, recover and reintegrate unconscious materials, so that the patient's life can become more satisfying.

Freud has been accused of thinking that all mental issues stem from the libido and repressed sexual urges and that his primarily one track mind being too rigid for an objective exploration of the human psyche. However, his contribution is much greater than that and without Freud many of the following theories and concepts that branched out from his thinking may never have evolved. Improving and expanding on great thought is the way of great theory and Freud paved the way for some great thinkers. Psychology owes Freud a great debt.

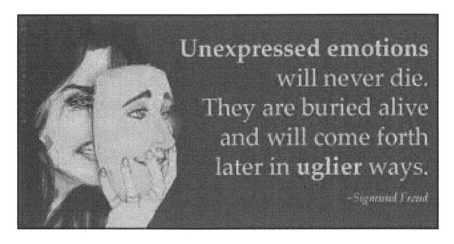

Freud in a nutshell – We are who we are due to repressed sexual urges and cultural conditioning. We can change.

Carl Gustav Jung

Mentored by Freud in his early career. Jung developed Freud's theory of the unconscious further. Discovering a personal unconscious made up of a shadow, an animus or anima, a deep and authentic (true) Self and many bit part players. Working extensively with dreams Jung developed theories about the collective unconscious which extended beyond the individual psyche and to which we all have access. Jung also used the term libido to describe a more general psychic energy as opposed to purely sexual.

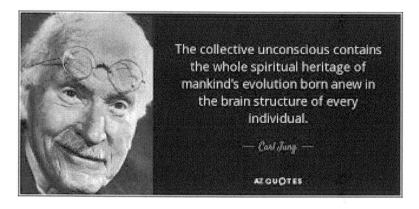

Jung developed basic natural principles (laws) that operate in the psyche.

- Every aspect of the psyche has a natural opposite that must be accepted and balanced.
- Equal energy is given to each of the opposites, meaning it is impossible to ignore one side of any opposite.

So for an example – one needs to give equal energy to our masculine and feminine energies acknowledging that our psyches are large and contain much that needs to be reconciled for personal growth and good mental health. Balancing our psyches is the route towards wholeness. Although wholeness is not thought possible, the aim towards wholeness is a journey without end.

Jung thought dreams were important and may act as compensation for areas of distortion, bring back memories from the collective unconscious and draw attention to both inner and outer aspects of our lives. A dream can arise from many different sources but it is always relevant and each dream is personal to the individual and can have symbolic links to society. Dreams are a communication between the unconscious and conscious minds.

Jung identified introversion (psychic energy turned inwards) and extraversion (psychic energy turned outwards) and combined with the four different functions called thinking, feeling, sensing and intuition produced Jungian typology. A great way of knowing your personality type and understanding both your behaviour and the behaviour of others. Understanding always lead to a more compassionate relationship with yourself and others. This is an invaluable tool for personal growth. I will discuss this more further on.

1. Jung's ideas about the collective unconscious and archetypes have given us new insights into the human psyche. And a knowledge of what the unconscious might contain.
2. His dream theories have expanded our understanding of the unconscious and the exploration of what could be called the unchartered region of our inner space. Unlocking tremendous possibilities. Jung opened up our inner space the way space

travel opened up outer space. We can all be space travellers to our inner space.

3. Jung's typology has become part of everyday thinking when dealing with personality types. Allowing us to know ourselves and others better. Do you know yourself? This was one of my defining moments, to discover both myself and others.

4. Jung's theory on the balancing of opposites allows us to achieve greater integration in the psyche towards individuation (wholeness). We always contain both opposites and a healthy psyche accepts and balances the opposites.

5. The psyche has an innate urge towards wholeness, and every individual has a tendency toward self-development or individuation. A recurring theme in psychology.

SELF-REALIZATION

- Also called *individuation*
- Psychological rebirth
- Process of becoming an individual or a whole person
- Achieved realization of the self, minimized their persona, recognized their anima, and acquired balance between introversion and extraversion

6. Individuation is the process of personal development toward wholeness. It involves establishing a connection between the ego and the self, and integrating various parts of the psyche

(soul). Understanding personality type helps to develop the weaknesses or inferior parts of our typology toward wholeness.

7. Jung considered the full range of human thought and behaviour to contain data from spiritual experiences. He viewed mystical belief systems as important expressions of human aspirations and ideals. Some modern day examples might include films such as Star Wars, Lord of the Rings and other mythical tales. A practice called movie yoga is the watching of these films with a view to reaping the deeper meaning from the tales. The hero is always thought to be the ego and the supporting cast other parts of the human psyche. A dragon could signify suffering or one's own primal urges to be battled and tamed. It is worth remembering that we are drawn to certain themes for an unconscious reason and that the movies originate in the human psyche. It all originates in the human mind, possibly the collective mind.

8. He called the images archetypes and they can be seen in many cultures and during many historical eras, as evidenced by common themes in world myths, folktales and legends such as the ones mentioned above.

We will touch on Jungian theory much more in my work. Jung's influence has extended worldwide; he is now widely accepted as one of the greatest thinkers of the 20th century.

Alfred Adler

Adler also networked with Freud early in his career but his theories of behaviour being driven by power as opposed to sexual energies developed away from those of Freud and a parting was inevitable. Nevertheless, we can further formulate an idea about the extent of Freud's influence as schools of thought branch off with new theories being explored.

For Adler, virtually all progress is the result of our attempts to compensate for inferiority feelings, the inferiority complex. These feelings motivate us in our most significant achievements. For example – Napoleon became a great leader due to his lack of physical stature. An extreme example of short guy syndrome. We progress by wanting more power (will to power).

In total opposition to Freud, Adler emphasised the pull of the future rather than the past for shaping personality. Where we hope to go is more important than where we have been.

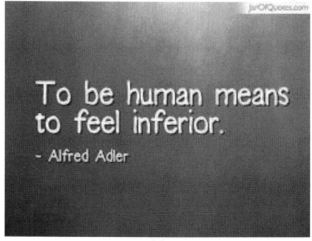

Adler thought that those personalities that have contributed most to humanity have been the most cooperative individuals, and the works of genius have always been oriented in a social direction. Only by functioning as cooperative, contributing members of society can we each overcome our actual inferiorities or our sense of inferiority. All behaviour happens in a social context. People cannot be studied in isolation.

Basic principles

1. The central motivation for each individual is lack, to strive for perfection or for superiority. This is the will to power. The goal of superiority or perfection motivates healthy individuals to seek continuous improvement and growth. Such striving is positive if it includes social concerns and interest in the welfare of others. It is negative if the focus is on personal superiority through domination of others

2. The individual is confronted by many life choices, He or she may choose healthy, socially useful goals or neurotic, socially useless ones. There is always a choice.

3. Behaviour is not determined by the past and repressed memories but by either heredity or the environment, usually both. Individuals are motivated by self-selected goals, which they feel will bring them success and happiness.

4. The self is the individual's style of life. It is the personality viewed as an integrated whole. Who we see when we look in the mirror is the product of our experiences and our choices.

5. The individuals attempt to compensate for inferiority feelings either imagined or real result in virtually all progress and

underlie humankinds most significant achievements. They can also result in self-hate through feelings of failure and inadequacy due to not being as we should be.

6. To become a worthy human being is a goal of the individual. Life's supreme law is that the diminishment of the sense of self-worth is not to be allowed. Easy to say – difficult to achieve.

7. The healthy individual is cooperative, has strong social interest, and constructively strives for superiority and power. This could also describe dictators.

 Karen Horney

Most of the early psychologists did not really understand women and viewed women as men that were lacking a penis or weren't interested enough in women to study them much at all. It makes sense to include a woman in this section. One of the first relevant women to take on the task of studying the human mind. It has to be understood how much harder it would have been for Karen Horney to enter this arena when a woman's place was still considered to be quietly in the home. She did however excel and is still relevant to this day amongst a male dominated field. Horney's influence can be seen in Maslow's work on self-actualisation.

Horney came to many of her theories through self-analysis. For example, she was intrigued by one of Adler's accounts of the masculine protest that develops in every woman in response to her sense of physical inferiority to men. At that time (early 1900's) she had no difficulty identifying the masculine protest in herself.

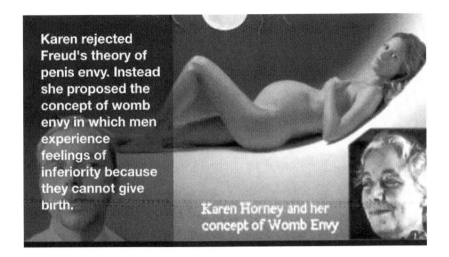

Karen rejected Freud's theory of penis envy. Instead she proposed the concept of womb envy in which men experience feelings of inferiority because they cannot give birth.

Karen Horney and her concept of Womb Envy

She envied Berndt because he could stand near a tree and pee, she liked wearing trousers (pants), played the prince in charades and at the age of 12 cut off her hair to the neckline. She compensated for her physical inferiority to males by excelling in school, taking great pride in being a better student than her brother. In terms of her culture, she was behaving like a man by studying medicine and believing in sexual freedom. According to Horney's self-analysis, she needed to feel superior because of her lack of beauty and her feminine sense of inferiority, which led her to excel in in a male domain. Could feminine personality be created by the masculine presence? Horney could see how such dynamics were real in shaping personality. It has since been widely accepted since that others presence in general affects behaviour. Sartre named it "being-for-others". We become who we are largely for others. The awakening process is largely dependent on this discovery and the subsequent efforts to find ourselves.

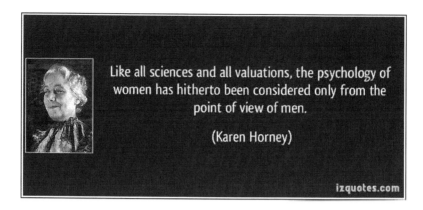

Like all sciences and all valuations, the psychology of women has hitherto been considered only from the point of view of men.

(Karen Horney)

izquotes.com

Basic principles

1. Horney was one of the founders of humanistic psychology, which is based on her emphasis that healthy values and the goals of life grow from self-realisation. Drawing on her own experience, she believed in the human potential for progress and growth and recognised the difficulty of achieving it. Horney built as bridge between formal psychology and self-help.

2. Horney acknowledged that she was deeply indebted to the foundation Freud provided. However, she came to see the male bias in psychoanalysis as reinforcing and reproducing the devaluation of the feminine. Simply put men did not really bother to include women in their theories except as an afterthought.

3. She proposed a women's view of the disturbances in the relations between the sexes and the differences between men and women, and suggested that girls and women must understand their patterns of development in their own terms,

not simply in relation to those of men. Horney made women visible in their own right.

4. Horney saw that it was the male position of privilege more than the penis that women envied, and that greater opportunity to develop their human capacities is needed for both men and women. Freud had positioned women as men with no penis, and admitted that he didn't understand women.

5. Horney proposed that all human beings have the innate tendency to self-realisation. This is a recurring theme amongst theorists under such headings as individuation, self-actualisation, enlightenment and salvation and is the energy that fuels the self-help industry. We all want to get better, to progress and to develop. I firmly believe this drive is how human beings evolve and constantly transcend what they were before. We are here to transcend our parents and be the best that we can be. This raises the energy level of the planet and that is how we make a difference every moment of every day.

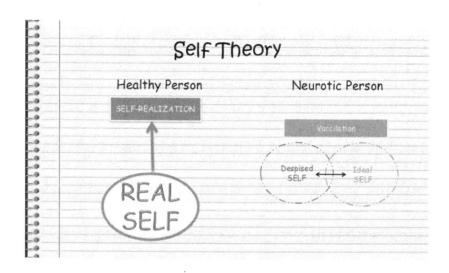

6. As our energies shift from developing our real potentialities to actualising our grandiose conception of ourselves, our behaviour is marked by the formation of the idealised image. This in turn, generates self-hate due to feelings of failure and inadequacy bought on by the great expectations not being realised.

Horney proposed that self-hate was the result not being what we "should" be as opposed to what we actually are. The "should" arises from our feelings of inadequacy and failure and is not real. This is a case of expecting too much from ourselves based on others expectations of how we should be, most often our significant others. In turn their urgings have arisen from their unlived lives that they have projected on to others. This in turn leads to neurosis which is a major stumbling block to self-realisation but nevertheless surmountable with awareness and work.

The Psychodynamic Theorists

Carl Jung

Highlighted universal themes in the unconscious as a source of creativity and insight. Found opportunities for personal growth by finding meaning in moments of coincidence.

Alfred Adler

Focused on the fight against feelings of inferiority as a theme at the core of personality, although he may have been projecting from his own experience.

Karen Horney

Criticized the Freudian portrayal of women as weak and subordinate to men.

She highlighted the need to feel secure in relationships.

In her book "**self-analysis**"(1942) , HORNEY outlined the 10 neurotic needs she had identified:

1. The Neurotic Need for Affection and Approval

2. The Neurotic Need for a Partner Who Will Take Over One's Life

3. The Neurotic Need to Restrict One's Life Within Narrow Borders

4. The Neurotic Need for Power

5. The Neurotic Need to Exploit Others

6. The Neurotic Need for Prestige

7. The Neurotic Need for Personal Admiration

8. The Neurotic Need for Personal Achievement

9. The Neurotic Need for Self-Sufficiency and Independence

10. The Neurotic Need for Perfection and Unassailability

There is of course much more to the work of Freud, Jung, Adler and Horney and there is a lot of literature on all of them if your appetite has been whetted by this rather brief introduction. Check the website for book leads www.adamsenex.com.

 Mind - Energy in Image Form - Jung's Archetypes

Although the subject of Archetypes is a very complex and rich topic, now might be a good moment to briefly define what the concept of archetypes is. Consider this an introduction of the briefest kind and bear with me if you are already well versed in Jung's archetypes.

Archetypal forms shape our thoughts, attitudes and ideas as ways of understanding our deeper selves. The parts of us that control our lives, not that they are separate from us but merely that we are initially largely unconscious of their presence and the affect they exert on our lives. Often called our unconscious or unconscious. A part of us that can be our worst enemy or our greatest ally. The way I look at it I choose the latter and think of my unconscious as my true on-board soul mate. In my thoughts there is no point in not valuing that which is a part of us and being our mind it makes sense to align with it personally and universally as I doubt we really have much choice. We can work with or against it, or as many of us do just ignore it and hope for the best. Even though we don't seem to speak the same language as our unconscious minds in the 21st century I am sure we can learn to communicate. Jung does provide a starting point to begin the sizeable task of really getting to know that unconscious part of our minds that contains all we have buried (shadow) and so much more through universal mind. Our minds are where our limitations are to be found, some would say have been deliberately planted and also where we may be able to disable the limiter. Let us be clear, we are controlled by our oppressors of that there can be little doubt once we begin to explore what happens behind our backs and stop accepting all of the crap we have swallowed since birth and for past generations of humanity.

Our unconscious mind communicates to us through dreams and images. These images are archetypes such as Puer (youth) and Senex (wise old man). Appearing in varying forms independently to humans all over the world with no apparent connection other than being a human being on this earth. They appear in dreams, myths, tales and images from the four corners of the earth and at different periods in the earth's history. You will recognise many of the stories, they are transforming energies represented by consistent images communicating to our conscious selves. They are not to be taken literally or read as part of history which has sadly happened with many for social control. In actual fact when made literal and historicised these valuable teaching tools lose much of their power and become a device for manipulation and control. They are intended to be fluid, ingested and understood for the personal deeper meanings relevant to self and collective as the energies within our psyche that they represent. We contain all of the energies (archetypes) in our psyches. Myths and archetypes speak to us differently depending on where we are at any given time in our psychic development. The myth shapes itself to the reader, as the dream speaks to the dreamer in the moment. No two people are the same and as such these communications are uniquely personal and relevant to us in that moment.

Archetypes / Collective Unconscious

• Archetypes = an unlearned tendency to experience things in a certain way (like a psychological instinct)

- *Persona* – our public face that we show to the world
- *Shadow* – the dark side of our personality
- *Anima* – feeling side of men; irrationality, moods
- *Animus* – thinking and reason in woman
- *Great* Mother – represents fertility/nourishment and destruction
- *Wise Old Man* – represents wisdom and knowledge
- *Hero*- powerful person who is part God, part human
- *Self* – disposition to move towards growth, perfection
  • *Need to balance unconscious/conscious, anima/animus, shadow/persona*

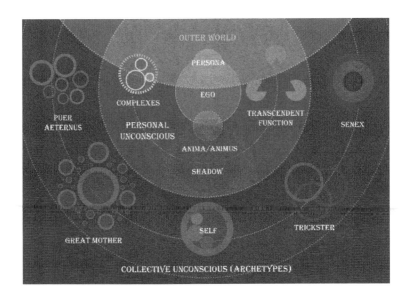

Myths are the world's dreams.
They are archetypal dreams and
deal with great human
problems. Myths and dreams
come from the same place. They
come from realizations of some
kind that then have to find
expression in symbolic form.

Joseph Campbell

PICTUREQUOTES.com

PICTUREQUOTES

It could be argued that the only authentic guide for a human
seeking truth is to be found in dreams, myth, tales and archaeology
away from the biased self-serving narratives we accept as fact from

the many manipulating political, scientific and religious institutions found across the world. There is more truth to be discovered in myth than any world news report. Now they truly are evil fairy tales. Our unconscious minds may already know and be connected to all we need to know, if only we can learn, or relearn a common form of communication between conscious and unconscious mind and stay clear of all distractions and brainwashing that keeps us from ourselves. The communication we are searching for may already be in use against us. Being open minded and expecting communication from our unconscious is the start.

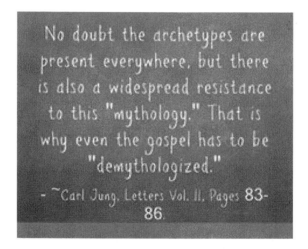

No doubt the archetypes are present everywhere, but there is also a widespread resistance to this "mythology." That is why even the gospel has to be "demythologized."
- ~Carl Jung, Letters Vol. II, Pages 83-86.

We can never hear if we are not listening or at least on the lookout for meaning. I have heard it stated that we should **never go to sleep without making a request to our unconscious mind.** We have all inadvertently tested this theory by dropping off with a preferred time for getting up in our heads and waking up at that time with no alarm. I do the same thing regularly in the daytime by being certain places on time. I do not wear a watch, I just let a time or event cross my mind and let it go and it seems to work out just fine for parcel deliveries and other visits to my house, I often return from my walks at the exact time they arrive. This may sound strange to our conditioned thinking but I have come to believe that the less I stress or care about the event the more likely it is to happen. In fact, to totally forget seems to work best and then I am surprised but smile as it has become more than a coincidence over the last few years. It works and the decision then is what do we need to know or ask for. Maybe just ask is there anything we need to know or for our dreams to be clear and mind expanding. Or even for extra help in understanding. The list grows as we think about how any communication could be improved. Just think about something important to us as we are drowsy and falling asleep.

Chilled Demons & Cheeky Heroes

Most of us are raised in a black and white world where opposites are opposites and never the twain shall meet. We are expected to be either one or the other with no bridge between. However, in experiencing life and being more self-aware it soon becomes obvious that grey is the prevailing colour and that in reality opposites are just the extremes of a continuum along which all of us find ourselves, neither all black or all white. Each of us in a position unique for us. There is no average or mean best place for all, it is different for each of us. We are all exceptions to the rule.

What helped me was the discovery some years back that when faced with opposites that accepting both is the wise decision, in fact

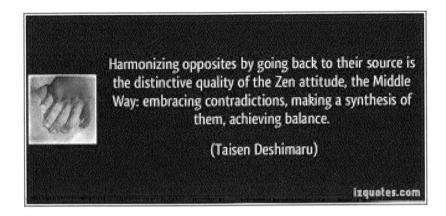

Harmonizing opposites by going back to their source is the distinctive quality of the Zen attitude, the Middle Way: embracing contradictions, making a synthesis of them, achieving balance.

(Taisen Deshimaru)

izquotes.com

even a good philosophy for living one's life by. We are faced with many value contradictions in trying to live our lives, possibly

religious against practical society values. Which way do we turn, do we have to choose, what is best for us and others? The practical values of Eating, earning, sex and winning at all costs set against the religious values of fasting, giving, celibacy and losing but playing the game right. These are all contradictions that we are living with every day from the moment we become conscious. It becomes more obvious looking at these examples that each of us must find a place somewhere in between that is just right for us, as trying to live up to external expectations or living the extremes will simply not work for most of us living in a society. List the four examples to yourself as a life philosophy right now. If you live in the western world in a capitalist economy the first four practical values may even seem like noble values. They are not. There are not enough mountain tops available to live out the religious extreme and as for the practical values, the path is set for self-destruct taking as many people with you as possible. The shadow looms

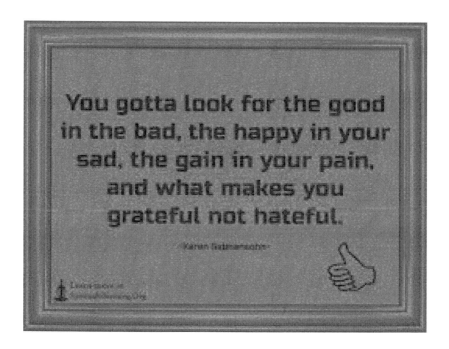

large for either extreme choice. Sadly, the practical list is what many young and old people strive for in our society. The second list often the cause for jokes. Is there a case for finding some middle ground? I would argue that it is imperative for humanity to insist on the middle ground for themselves and their loved ones as the collective human shadow is destroying the planet and humanity. What we see on the news is largely the behaviour of collective shadow. The result of a worldwide philosophy for living that is not working at either extreme.

Coaching awareness, personal progress and generally purposefully getting better at being who we are, it would be easy for me to mislead or fool my readers and myself by allowing us all to assume that we are expected to be perfectly good and eliminate all that is perceived to perfectly bad from within us. For us to expect all actions and thoughts to be good (whatever that is) and perfect (ditto) would in fact be considered regressive and getting worse. Bear with me I will explain. Life is not so simple that we can view all things as black and white and choose which we prefer. We are far more complex beings. Attempting to be "all good" is attempting to deny who we are by repressing any traits or behaviours considered unbefitting to our goal of perfection. These become what Jung named our shadows and unrecognised are prone to reveal themselves from their unconscious home when we are least expecting it. Without recognition and inner work our shadow side will ensure we are anything but "all good" or perfect. We are human, to be human is to work with our imperfections, fully aware of their existence. The title of this section and this book is descriptive of how I like to approach my psyche, by accepting we

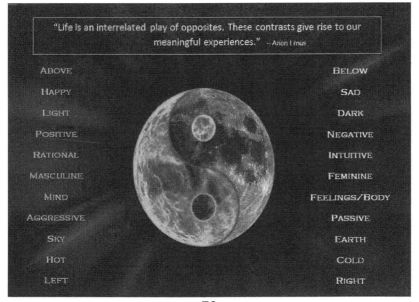

"Life is an interrelated play of opposites. These contrasts give rise to our meaningful experiences." - Anon I mus

ABOVE	BELOW
HAPPY	SAD
LIGHT	DARK
POSITIVE	NEGATIVE
RATIONAL	INTUITIVE
MASCULINE	FEMININE
MIND	FEELINGS/BODY
AGGRESSIVE	PASSIVE
SKY	EARTH
HOT	COLD
LEFT	RIGHT

contain all pairs of opposites in our psyche to some degree, there is no light without dark.

I can then begin to accept myself as I appear to others and start to work on the very interesting lifetime task of getting know myself. That is not to imply that I am particularly interesting but rather that any discovery about ourselves and what makes us tick behind our backs would be considered interesting to any of us. It is the discovery that we are all so much more than we have been led to believe to this point and that our personal and collective potential is, as yet, untapped. We have our curiosity piqued and a purpose for the rest of our lives to attempt to transcend our current, often very low expectations of ourselves. Awareness means that the comfortable automaton life is to all intents and purposes now over and life in search of meaning leading to personal and collective progress has begun.

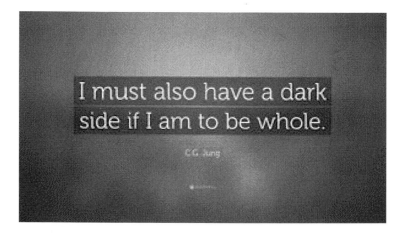

I must also have a dark side if I am to be whole.

C.G. Jung

The ideal vision for me is one in which my darker shadow side (there is positive in shadow also) which I playfully call my villain or demon I react to in a chilled and accepting manner, whilst my "all good" ego/persona or my hero has a cheeky side. I view all opposites as being on a continuum and work to find the middle ground or at least avoid extremes. This helps to appreciate more realistically who I am by balancing ego inflation with any probable shadow attacks. Ideally I see my charming demons and cheeky heroes as one fully aligned, loving and accepting energetic entity, which is kind of what it is. There is place rarely visited where our heroes and demons are "just right". A place where I for one wish to spend as much time as possible in whatever future I have in store, much of which depends on matters such as how I cope with my shadow and how I align my persona, shadow and authentic self.

Before my awareness improved I had unpreparedly experienced my shadow in a particularly low point in my life and I would rather have it as a friend than an enemy. Although the many shadow moments have taught me much about myself and the very real existence of my shadow energy and the damage that can be done against our conscious will. Shadow is a reoccurring theme in my books and the line I like that explains this perfectly is that "what we don't know can hurt us", and will unless we make it our business to know ourselves better. Our shadow is responsible for all that is suffering and "unlucky" in our lives. "It always happens to me", those out of character moments often put down to tiredness or stress are your unconscious shadow living you. Once we begin to become more aware it does illuminate how our unconscious behaviours are ruling our lives and then we can start to work on them with a loving acceptance as opposed to denying and repressing them until they surface without our knowledge or any control. Often with disastrous consequences.

Realistic Character Continuum

~~Pure Villain~~←-----(Charming Demons & Cheeky Heroes)-----→~~Pure Hero~~

[<----Just Right-->]

The realisation and widespread acceptance that there is an unconscious aspect of ourselves has basically changed the pursuit of self-awareness. It is widely accepted that we have aspects to our minds that we are only now becoming more aware of. We have a conscious side that we are familiar with (ego or persona) and an unconscious side about which we are personally clueless but is no mystery to others that see its behaviours regularly and it influences us beyond our awareness. We are wonderfully ignorant of the fact that when observing others, we are often observing a side of them that they are blissfully unaware of and vice versa. And we may even be watching a projection of ourselves in others and finding it distasteful. Totally oblivious to the fact that we are seeing our own shadow projected away. What better place to hide?

Hypocrisy (Wikipedia)

- Also, some people genuinely fail to recognize that they have character faults which they condemn in others.
- This is called psychological projection.
- This is self-deception rather than deliberate deception of other people.
- In other words, "psychological hypocrisy" is usually interpreted by psychological theorists to be an unconscious defense mechanism rather than a conscious act of deception, as in the more classic connotation of hypocrisy.

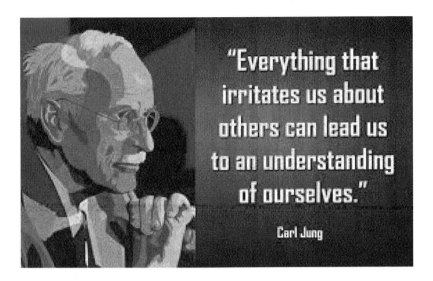

"Everything that irritates us about others can lead us to an understanding of ourselves."

Carl Jung

We can begin to understand how this works by knowing ourselves and others better, by knowing our personality tendencies and their opposites, we can begin to know persona and what may contribute to our shadow side.

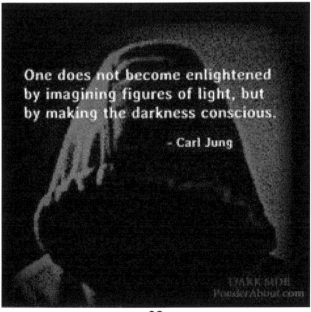

One does not become enlightened by imagining figures of light, but by making the darkness conscious.

- Carl Jung

Knowing You and I

Jung's typology is the result of the work of Carl Gustav Jung and part of Jungian psychology. Often copied and imitated Jung's typology is one of the worlds most established and well respected models on personality and behaviour and can help us to know and understand ourselves and others better if never completely as we are always in fluid process and ever changing. I know from personal experience it has been a revelation for me in learning to understand both myself and particularly Julie, my wife, better. I am far less judgemental and more accepting of both myself and others thanks to Jung. I would say never judgemental but only a fool would expect that once aware of the dangers of expecting any one-sided perfection with a shadow lurking in the unconscious full of the discarded opposite. Long having been controversially and commercially adapted for recruitment and career planning, by matching personality type to suited vocations. A task that may be okay temporarily but due to the fluid nature of personality, extremely doubtful long term. Personality can never be cast in stone, given a label and then that is it for ever. We all change within our types, within different situations and across time. I know that within my type I have many moments of the opposite and others would never know my type, at times I still question it. But I just go back to times when I did not have so many personas created and there I can find myself before I donned so many of my disguises and armour. We contain all there is but tend to favour certain aspects as more natural and less draining. Typology can be, and is best used as intended by Jung as one's personal guide in expanding our self-awareness, in relating with better understanding to the significant people in our lives, in our creativity and most importantly in living comfortably according to our own true nature – without apology or regret – knowing how our psychology works within us according to our essential nature is a revelation. I know it explained much for me and provided healing, self-acceptance and great relief after decades of holding myself up to unrealistic standards put in place by our oppressive controllers for control and profit. We spend too much time working to be someone we are not to fit all kinds of situations in work, rest and play. Typology allows us to know and accept more readily our strengths and weaknesses and to know better to which situations we are naturally suited and to which a special effort and greater energy expenditure may be needed.

We may discover we are drawn to some people and have found others difficult or impossible to relate to up to this point. Why we are attracted to certain activities and avoid others like the plague, why a certain relationship isn't working, or why we dislike certain aspects of our job more than others or find certain aspects more energy draining. We can make choices that truly suit who we are and communicate with others with more depth, understanding and effectiveness. We begin to see our worlds more clearly and much of our history makes sense at last. We can then be more realistic in our expectations and test our limitations out in the world in a more controlled and progressive way towards self-expansion, rather than getting in too deep and diminishing ourselves. Once I began studying personality typology it explained my relationship with Julie very well, there were many eureka moments. We are an attraction of opposites. The credibility for Jung's typology came from the truths that it revealed for me after the fact. I had lived the life and felt the truth of the explanation for the life I had experienced. It was an Oh wow! Moment. Over 30 years ago there was a strong drive for me to be with Julie, over and above the normal attraction drive. I always thought the same old crap and that it was meant to be but I was not sure why. But the power of that initial attraction and drive has stuck with me as strange to this day. This feeling is even what kept us together for me when our world was turned upside down and splitting up would have been the sensible choice, or at least the easiest at that time. It would seem that my unconscious mind doesn't do common sense and intuition was the winner. There was definitely something keeping us together above and beyond the call of logic. Forces at work that I don't understand. As it turns out our unconscious minds decided to take a short cut to psychic wholeness and found what each of us was lacking in another person. This happened at a level that neither of us were aware of but I was aware that the situation was a little bit special and a little confused. There are mysteries that we may never fully understand and even this meaning that I now comfortably attribute to my situation may be miles of the mark. It is funny that being opposites is what unknowingly attracted us but as seems to be the norm for any couple we then tried to change the other to be more like ourselves. This plainly is not a great idea and it took us about 25 years to realise our mistake. Now we are aware we can both accept the other and work on those aspects of ourselves that are lacking whilst being grateful for the presence of the other. We have the added benefit of ongoing support and teaching by example of the other to ensure our success. It works. All we have to do is look at the other and work on those aspects of them that we find alien to ourselves.

Understanding definitely fosters love. To be living with a flesh and blood example is almost the perfect scenario for getting better and towards becoming totally self-reliant. That being said, it is still not easy to introduce what feel like unnatural behaviours into our lives. Perhaps the greatest gain is in allowing others to be themselves through the understanding of their psychology and of psychology in general. Not living with the expectation of just one right way to be is in itself liberating. No longer expecting others to interact with the world in ways that are quite possibly contrary to their nature at this time. We are both changing, getting better in ways that expand who we are rather than diminish ourselves to fit others and society expectations.

Jung's typology allows for the very real possibility of harmonising different personalities for the benefit of all involved through awareness and understanding of self and others and not expecting everyone to be like us when difference is natural and must be celebrated across the board. We are all the exception to the rule.

Two important questions concerning personality.

1. Do you know who you are?
2. Are you living your own way, authentically?

Jung's typology and our own conscious efforts will bring us closer to our own personal truth.

I have no intention of dealing in detail with typology here in this book as others have done that better than I ever could, however I would like to discuss just a small part of it to illustrate the difference this knowledge can make to our lives and to give you examples of how it works in reality from my life. I will briefly discuss introversion and extraversion and would like to reiterate here that we are not introverted or extraverted but rather contain both with tendencies to be more one than the other. I repeat this because I witness constantly people announcing that they are one or the other. I am guilty of this also and it is a hard habit to break. Attaching a label that then becomes a self-fulfilling prophecy. I hate labels and I have on more than one occasion introduced myself as an introvert rather than as a man being prone to introversion. I can do a pretty good extravert at times also but I am sure that will never become a habit as it is just not as comfortable or natural and there are situations that I have never (yet) been able to overcome, such as dancing in plain view for all to see and judge.

Never dance naked because the body has parts that do not stop moving when the music stops!

I consider myself prone to introversion going well back into my childhood but I will never limit myself to being only an introvert with all that is included. I want to leave the door open to choose myself at any given moment. I want to explore the mysterious kingdom of extraversion where my wife likes to live.

 Extravert, Introvert or Ambivert

Introversion ←----------------Ambivert----------------→ Extraversion

> *There is no such thing as a pure introvert or extrovert. Such a person would be in the lunatic asylum.* – Jung

Ambivert is the term used for the vast majority of us that display both extravert and introvert tendencies. However, this can be a little confusing as using myself as an example I am no stranger to either tendency but I most definitely favour introversion. The danger of the term ambivert is that it may neutralise the whole concept. I am not sure of the value of including it here but on reflection decided it is worth having it here though just to illustrate that this is a continuum and as such a fluid process where either extreme is doubtful and the need to understand the concept in its entirety is important to us rather than just picking out the part we think may affect us. As usual we contain it all in different measures with most of us fluctuating according to the situation but preferring one end of the scale as our more natural tendency.

I must warn against labelling once more as I have just seen an article where the writer has stated that they are 49% introverted 51% extraverted and as such the near perfect ambivert. I had to laugh as that would be impossible to know and is more likely to prove the writer unaware of themselves than of anything perfect. Maybe none of these three terms should be used as nouns, that might help. What is it with our need to label all that we know?

Ambiverts exhibit both extroverted and introverted tendencies. This means that they generally enjoy being around people, but after a long time this will start to drain them. Similarly, they enjoy solitude and quiet, but not for too long. Ambiverts recharge their energy levels with a mixture of social interaction and alone time.

I can't help but wondering if the category of ambiverts has evolved by necessity due to the pressures exerted by lifestyles in our society. Either extreme would cause problems so what better than introverts getting out more and some down time for extraverts to restore some much needed balance to the psyche. There would still be a tendency of one over the other and as such a more natural living style would evolve. Nobody is born comfortable with both.

Ambivert may be the name for the goal, the ideal, rather than an actual real state of mind.

In a nutshell ambiversion is what all of us will be exhibiting that are not at either end of the continuum full time. Ambiversion is that somewhere in between where all who are considered sane are to be found. Ambiversion does not exist without extraversion and introversion. It is not whether we can be or win at either it is where we feel in our souls that we are more comfortable. There is no prize for either, but there may be some progress in knowing where we are and getting better where we can and in understanding others.

Is the term ambiversion of any value. Maybe only if it is possible to be the perfect balance as one's true nature. Maybe not. You decide.

Let's get on with the important stuff.

Where do you put your attention and get your energy? Do you like to spend time in the outer world of people and things (Extraversion), or in your inner world of ideas and images (Introversion)?

 Extraversion

Extraverts are energised and comfortable around people, when stated that human beings are all gregarious they were obviously talking about extraverts. They love to spend time with others, as this is how they recuperate from spending time alone or hard at work. The term "being a people person" describes an extravert. They are at their most charged and passionate when they are around others. A quiet night in for them would entail about half a dozen friends or family and they just love spontaneous drop in visits. They love people. Some will love others with compassion and a genuine interest whilst for others company is like a fix and the opportunity to perform in front of an audience.

> I desperately need people. I recharge by sitting near those I love, laughing at their antics, and sharing stories. Being by myself is exhausting.

Extraverts are often lively, warm, funny and the life and soul of any gathering. They can also be very demanding, particularly for those more introverted. They love centre stage and are prepared to do anything to keep the spotlight on them. For many this is not a problem as they can be charming and very good company if a little intense. There is the possibility of them becoming a pain in the arse and needing to take a chill pill now and again.

Extraverts find it easy to meet new people, walking into most situations and comfortably chatting immediately. By the end of most gatherings they have made new contacts and swapped details for future social interactions, thus ensuring a constant supply of people to energise them. At the same time, they have probably ignored their partner as they have been too busy making new friends.

Extraverts do not like their own company and as such become bored very easily. Repetitive tasks will cause them to deflate unless they can be turned into something more interesting like the promise of attention or status for performing well. With the concentration span of a gnat (strange saying! How do they know?) compared to introverts.

They share their thoughts as they think them which can be very confusing as a conversation becomes others accompanying them in their thought process. Analysing out loud is par for the course for extraverts and as such what they say is often not the finished product or even close.

Extraverts tend to have a wide circle of friends, and will put a lot of energy into those friendships which are 'current'. They are not particularly picky with who they are friends with, quantity over quality every time. All may join the party. They have many friends but their definition of a friend is very different to that of an introvert but nevertheless rewarding for all parties.

 Introverts.

Introverts will love only a very few people in a lifetime and then only in small doses which they will need to control. Unexpected drop in visits are rarely welcomed no matter who you are, even if they are doing nothing. Nothing is a very real something to an extrovert.

Even when familiar with large groups of people introverts are not overly keen on too much attention. Okay in a bar seated with a group but likely to be either listening or engaged in a deep conversation with one, maybe two others. They often don't say much but when they do it is well thought out and worth listening to. Although quiet they can still enjoy their time, that is their way. The party is inside their heads.

The behaviour of an introvert is often similar to someone who is shy but shyness can be found in introverts and extraverts, there is no connection. An extravert may overcome shyness for singing or dancing with alcohol or drugs but no amount of either will change an introvert into a singer or dancer if that is how they are. I know this for sure as I have been pushed and prompted to join in dancing at clubs for years and years but whatever my physical state I have always felt uncomfortable and avoided what I consider to be the humiliation. Fine for others just not for me thanks. My biggest problem is often extraverts pressuring me to be like them, thinking I am miserable or boring because I don't feel the need to dance. I still love and feel music inside. I avoid social gatherings because of the feeling of being a misfit due to lack of understanding even though I now know better.

Introverts focus mainly on their own internal world and are quite oblivious to what is going on around them. My wife hoovering and the dogs barking, "How can you read a book with so much noise?" is the question. I don't even notice when I am engrossed. It is because whilst introverting we have an astounding knack for shutting the world out, and be happy in this self-imposed isolation. It is perfectly possible for an introvert to be lonelier in a crowded room, such as the social gatherings I mentioned previously than on their own. It can be very tiring to have to pay attention to other people for any length of time, an introverts definition of boring, but they can concentrate on 'things' that interest them for ages. They tend to pursue solitary hobbies and pastimes rather than seek to be involved in groups or team games. Introverts need engagement inside their heads.

Because of their cautious nature introverts can be painfully slow to develop relationships. When they do the relationship will be a strong one that often endures for the rest of their lives. They will have a small circle of close and trusted friends that they would do anything for, even if they don't see them from one year to the next. Introverts go for quality over quantity when choosing friends. Not needing to spend endless hours with friends to reinforce the relationship. They hate small talk, but appreciate the value of small talk for testing whether others are agreeable or not. However, the introvert hating small talk may well seem disagreeable when first experienced.

> "Part of the beauty of an Introvert/Extrovert team is having someone you know will handle the things that drain you."

Introverts are mostly like to keep their ideas to themselves until they have thought them through. They can be very uncomfortable being made to speak about something they are not sure about. An idea can percolate in an introvert's mind for a very long while until it evolves into something they consider worth sharing. Debating an unfinished idea is not their way of figuring something out, in fact it will distract and even confuse them.

In relationships they may not be forthcoming with their feelings, particularly verbally. Expecting that much can be assumed and left unsaid. They communicate better in letters and cards, or in gestures. Actions saying more than words. All is contained within for the introvert and they may need some prompting for it to reach the outside world at which time the depth may be astounding.

Developing an Understanding

Extraverts often describe introverts as boring 'Norman no mates', while they themselves are often described by more introverted others as shallow and loud. These perceptions can have a big effect in any kind of relationship.

This is the way it can work; introverts can get lonely when they are surrounded by people they don't know or in busy places. Extraverts get lonely when they are in their own company.

Introversion isn't antisocial, it is just that the social way is different and not considered normal in our extraverted society. Socialising will involve people that are known and the conversations may be deeper and in smaller groups or one to one. Listening and observing also plays a bigger part in the social life of an introverted person.

When a relationship between the two types exists there is a need for both to recognise each other's needs. The importance of privacy for introverts which will seem like solitary confinement to an extravert and the love of gatherings for extraverts which will feel like an invasion for introverts – no matter who the company.

Introverted behaviour is territorial. Introverts need their own space; private places both in their environment and in their mind which they will defend strongly. And maybe not the shed at the bottom of the garden as is depicted in many sitcoms. But that is better than having to face situations that are considered turbulent for an introvert.

Its funny how when Im loud, people tell me to be quiet, but when Im quiet, people ask me whats wrong with me.

Introverts in a relationship with an extravert need to be aware of the importance of arousal and stimulation. No matter how alien it may seem to them, their partner's focus is on the world outside of them, and as you may have gathered already, sameness becomes invisible and flattens an extraverted personality quicker than popping a balloon. An unchanging environment and life in general to an extrovert quickly becomes boring because of its lack of stimulation and the fact that it throws them back on their own inner resources and that is not where they like to live. It does not mean they are bored of their partner, only that there is not enough going on. Although it can lead to conflict unless both partners are aware of the other's needs. Some variation is needed, even some spontaneity in the social calendar. An awareness that both will benefit from a little of the others world is also vital. And there is much personal growth to be found in the attraction of such opposites. However, it does require working together with understanding. Another example showing that good relationships are never easy, but worth the effort.

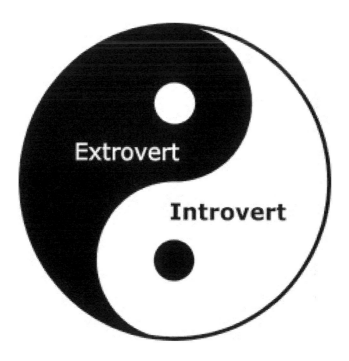

Extraverts are more open and one can see how the silence of an introvert could be misinterpreted by the extravert as deceitful or showing a lack of trust or a holding back from intimacy. It is difficult to understand that a person can be so different from ourselves but it is a fact. As with all opposites, there is the potential for each partner to balance the other and for the relationship to be mutually fulfilling and a learning experience for both. Open minded understanding not labelling from ones biased viewpoint is what is needed. Neither is right or wrong, good or bad, just different and very interesting. And we all have moments of the opposite type and are unaware because it is our unconscious shadow revealing itself. What better than our partners alerting us to our shadow moments.

Extraverts will not need to much prompting to talk about themselves with very little, make that no censorship. To extraverts an introvert will appear secretive. They will not usually talk about their problems When the extravert is sharing and the introvert is not this can make the relationship seem very one-sided. This will be the time when an introverted partner may appear the most withdrawn. With patience and understanding the introvert will learn to share more. As I have mentioned already with my 30+ year marriage, opposites attract and you will often find these two types in relationships, and they often complement each other. I will talk more about making it work when discussing how Julie and I benefit from one another. Although with such a fluid concept and many of us fluctuating between the two, the figures I have seen state that 75% of the population is extrovert, while 25% is introvert. It explains a lot about our culture, and everything about gameshows, reality television and the hunger for celebrity status which an introvert will find alien or fascinating at best. At least in the first part of life our society is made for extraverts and maybe the figures reflect that necessity for us to show extravert behaviours. I know I would say personally that I naturally have introversion tendencies as a boy and young man I showed all the signs but I became more extraverted in order to get through the first part of my life. I was pushed into situations by parents that assumed I would outgrow my personality as was the lot for introverts and maybe still is. All through my extravert years I was made to feel like I was strange for not wanting what others all obviously wanted. That is an extravert society and we must watch out for introverts more and realise and value the differences. I am now settled back into a mostly introverted personality style. The time for reflection comes to us all in the second part of our lives and that it would seem is when introverts come into their own.

I know Julie and I having knowledge of Jung's typology improved matters in my life when Julie grasped how unnatural it is for me to venture out into the world or how I opt so readily to being alone and Julie realises she is often my bridge to the outside world and I no longer fight my natural tendencies believing I am just boring or odd. In contrast I am Julie's "inner guide", both equally daunting places for the other. We are aware it is vital to be accepting of the others type and grateful for the support each of us lends in areas of potential discomfort. For me, it explains Julies hyper-willingness to "pop" here, there and everywhere at a moment's notice for human contact and for Julie, my need to plan and prepare for a trip to the local store. I have not actually made it to our local store in eighteen months of living here. Online shopping does makes introversion much easier. We are also aware that we can develop accordingly in order that we not be dependent on one another for our wholeness. It is a challenge to become more balanced by facing those situations that will expand us and it is good to know we have an understanding other to support our growth. This has not always been the case and our relationship has arrived at this point because of hard work, tenacity and eventually an awareness that there is so much more to us than the accepted norms. Different paths on a shared journey.

Previously in the first part of life I created a physique and fake personas a plenty to hide behind and see me through all kinds of situations. We all do that and it is important to develop a strong ego. Reflecting now, I never really fooled myself and I was mostly uncomfortable and struggled with many simple situations that I thought were because I was a little "special". Situations such as going to the bar for a drink in a pub or bar or any public situation that I thought exposed me to others and made me feel awkward. On the rare occasion that I overcame my fear I did feel exactly that, exposed and awkward. From my perspective, in a society where extraversion is the norm we need to understand introverts better and recognise their unique attitude and contribution to society. I firmly believe that Jung's personality typology should be taught in schools as part of mass education and to a degree that it is really understood, not used as a label of what is good or better than being another way. This would aid in mutual understanding and help young people find a place in the world at an early age as opposed to feelings of alienation and self-loathing in attempting to be what we are not. Or living in way that is unsuited to who we are to please significant others or a system that ignores a large section of the population. How many young people would be on a different path if they knew their real strengths and didn't grow up being led to believe they are weaknesses or abnormal behaviours?

If you have read book 1 of the series, you will know that I personally spent precious years of my life drinking too much and eventually taking drugs just to feel comfortable (numb) in an extravert's world. I reflect on the number of times I just felt invisible. How many of our children feel like this? I got lucky and chose life over death at the critical moments later in my life. Three of my friends made a different choice. Many are not so lucky and would love to become truly visible to their loved ones and others more aware of difference. There are fewer sadder feelings than being invisible to the ones you love and that purport to love you, simply because they are unaware of your needs compared to theirs or you feel like an oddity in an extravert's world, struggling to breathe. Jung's typology explained my life and my visibility to myself and Julie and importantly made Julie more visible to me. I am also much more accepting of others being just how they are as opposed to how I think they should be. I owe the quality of my life to psychology and to the genius of Carl Gustav Jung in particular.

Discovering and Accepting Your Shadow

The word shadow used to describe the unconscious part of our minds that we have discarded as not befitting who we are in our perceptions of ourselves, was first introduced to the public domain by Swiss Psychologist Carl Gustav Jung. Our shadow is the dumping ground for all those characteristics of our personalities that we disown. This is an essential part of the socialising process, without this ability we would be primitive and have no place in a cultured society. We are all born whole but culture demands that we display only part of our nature and refuse other parts of our genetic inheritance. In short our cultures demand we fragment our psyche in order to fit in with behavioural norms. Culture insists we rise above the simple human in us and demands a more cultivated public face. To oversimplify for the sake of clarity we are each divided into an ego (persona) and a shadow. The shadow not only contains bad stuff but it can contain good also. For instance, if a

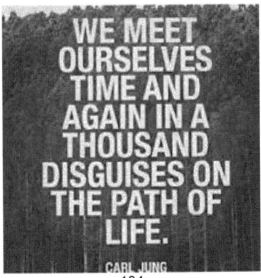

man has a reputation as a tough business man he would resign his benevolent side or at least aspects of it to his shadow. The same for any man rejecting his feminine side or woman rejecting her masculine traits. The only criteria are that the traits are unacceptable to the culture of the individual persona.

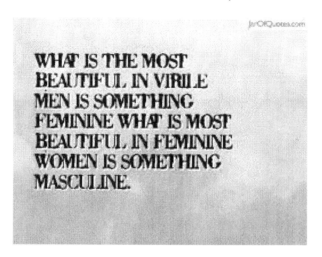

Ironically in the first half of our lives we seem to be intent on separation and providing our cultural needs and behaviours. Disciplining ourselves and constructing our personas to be just as we feel they need to be. Upon reaching the second half of our lives we then become devoted to restoring the wholeness to our natures that we were born with and then denied. The important thing is to balance our cultural personalities with our shadows. Personal effectiveness is balancing at the centre and producing only what can be countered by the other side. We must hide our dark side from society in general but we must never try to hide it from ourselves. A loving acceptance, a shadow, persona, healthy ego alignment is the perfect scenario. One cannot exist without the other.

The first half of life is devoted to forming a healthy ego,

The second half is going inward and letting go of it.
Carl Jung

You can identify your shadows by looking at what you project onto others. When you deny a trait in yourself, you tend to be very aware of that trait in other people. In the twelve-step tradition, they say, "If you spot it, you got it." This means that you are most aware of those traits in others which reflect your own shadows. You may react irrationally to one of these traits in someone else, becoming unduly annoyed and blowing things all out of proportion. If others emotionally affect you, you should look deeper. If you are merely observing them, then that is not a problem.

Shadow work is about transforming energies. We have lots of energy in our bodies and surrounding us. Names, such as prana, life-energy, chi, libido and Eros are but a few of the identifications for such energies that largely remain a mystery to modern medicine. Alternative treatments are more open-minded in this

106

respect. Anger is loaded with energy that can be accepted and transformed rather then played out or regressed. Never feeling fear, anger or stress would be a worry and a recipe for an explosion of emotions or physical ailments caused by these repressed emotions. Recognising these emotions as natural and working to transform the energy is the healthy option and where the real growth is to be found.

Nobody said it would be easy, it requires becoming conscious of rising emotions in order that they can be controlled and transformed in a positive way. Emotions that are often in control of us and that have previously unconsciously risen and taken hold before we can react in a way that we would consciously choose. Getting a grip in these moments of unconscious possession is the key to transformation. It begins when we think about such moments and accept responsibility for our actions, with repetition this starts building a new programme in our unconscious. A programme that we have chosen. The act of transforming is in itself an extremely motivating experience and motivation then becomes a big part of the transformation.

An example of this transformation process in the real world would be that precious moment when we are overcome with rage and out of the blue something makes us laugh and try as we might (unconsciously) we can't remain serious and in a rage. We can't help but giggle like school children. We all need to giggle like school children more often. What an awesome way to transform energy, the feeling is wonderful. And as an added bonus our ego may suffer a well needed moment of humility and we may feel just a little silly for overreacting in the first place.

It can help a lot to have visions that we can call upon to stop our anger in its tracks. A funny scene or a loving moment, whatever it takes to shift the energy from negative and destructive to positive and constructive.

The fact is to acknowledge as a core belief that no matter how right we feel we are (ego), anger does nobody any good if used destructively or repressed, least of all our own selves. The giggling example shows how easy it can be done once we begin making the choice to deal with our emotions in such a way that we develop our personality in that moment. It is far wiser to be kind to others and ourselves than to be right and by developing love for ourselves and others we will find this task becoming second nature quite soon. Start by loving yourself. A great place to begin. If we do have aggressive tendencies than exercise is a fantastic way to transform negative energy towards positive ends. Don't deny your shadow just find ways to accommodate it and make progress in every way.

If you have read my earlier books, particularly the first, "*Dazed and Confused*" you will know that I went through a period in my life when I had little or no control over my rage. Insanely I always managed to justify it to myself. A dangerous practice. Fortunately for me the damage was contained and I realised my regressive tendencies could have no positive outcome my whole life was the opposite to my writing philosophy – My philosophy now is to champion awareness, progress and getting better - *I write about awareness, progress, getting better and how that might work for us all in the real world. My writing by necessity is probably more rebel than Zen* – Previously I lived my life with no awareness, regression and getting worse. All that I came into contact with at that time turned to shit (excuse me). I was a master at creating a shitty life out of the blue. The law of attraction working in the negative perfectly. But I woke up, and only just in time. I have used exactly the methods I write about to conquer my demons or maybe we never conquer our demons but rather understand a little better, make friends and allies of them thus keeping them from taking over our lives. Chilling our demons.

There is a key moment in every emotional situation and I learned to win that moment with love initially for myself, breathing techniques and walking away until the rage subsided and could be dealt with consciously. I learned to recognise when I was acting unconsciously and I chose to take responsibility in the moment rather than make excuses after the damage was done. With perseverance the rages stopped entirely with the eventual acceptance that nothing is worth the pain and suffering caused by destructive unconscious emotions. It was hard and I still have that particular shadow waiting in the wings but I know him well now and we work together these days. We are brothers in my psyche and he is my chilled demon and I have become a cheeky hero for myself. Awareness is the most important value you will ever develop. Once aware I just surrendered. I let go of the struggle and guess what? My life just transformed, the rages had made me blind to what life can be like. I count myself lucky to get the opportunity to learn and grow. I got a second chance in my life. My life had changed with my thinking and still today my life follows my thoughts and my deep unconscious expectations. And for the record it is only the awareness that keeps me form lapsing back into less than precious moments. The possibility is always there amongst all of the possible reactions and outcomes in every situation. I just make better choices now than I did previously.

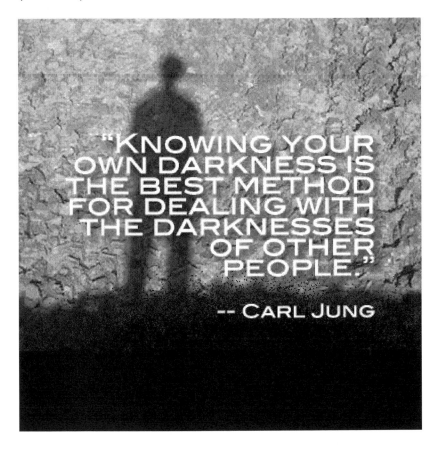

I believe my rage (shadow) developed from years of being taught to turn the other cheek and being "good". A gentle giant. Nowadays I work with my shadow side to create balance. I no longer choose the obvious good over its opposite. I merely accept the presence of both and control them on a psychological level. I balance my light and dark sides in the knowledge that neither can exist without the other. For me getting better meant wanting to be the best I can be by acknowledging the worst I can be and fusing them together. I have reached the stage that I can now laugh at my dark thoughts and some of my actions knowing that I am ultimately in charge of choosing who I am in this world. I have outlets such as the gym or out in nature where I can vent my shadow side or I can whinge to Julie and that always ends up with a giggle. I no longer berate myself for having the full set of demons and heroes. My goal? Charming Chilled Demons & Cheeky Heroes.

 Narcissistic Personality Disorder

It should be noted that all people are somewhat narcissistic as it helps with one's survival instinct if you put yourself first at least some of the time. Pathological Narcissists are not aware of others. This may be the single biggest threat to humanity should all egos develop as narcissistic selves. Separation and a world devoid of love are the guaranteed result of a world ruled by the narcissist.

The word narcissism has taken on an almost comedy meaning for people that are self-centred or vain. And as such it is an underestimated foe that we have to deal with. In actual fact I have heard it described by Erich Fromm as the single biggest threat to mankind.

An understanding of this irrational behaviour has surfaced. The dictionary definition of narcissism is actually very poor – "Excessive or erotic interest in oneself and one's physical appearance." A better definition is an orientation in which all one's interest and passion are directed to one's own person: One's body, mind, feelings, interests and so forth. For the narcissistic person only they and what concern them are fully real. What concerns others is real only in a superficial sense only inasmuch as it affects them. They have no love, no compassion, and no rational objective judgment. The narcissistic person is often accused of loving themselves when they in fact are incapable of loving others or themselves. The narcissist has built an invisible wall around themselves. And they are expert at constructing disguises for themselves so as to seem anything but narcissist, the condition is known as one of the most difficult of psychic qualities to discover. The issue is that you never can tell a genuine reaction from an ego driven reaction designed to control others this makes attending and understanding the narcissist extremely difficult if not impossible. Also, a narcissist will get a fix from arguing or fighting as much as from any caring attention. Attention it would seem is all the same to a narcissist. The fear is in not being noticed or totally ignored. Simple things like loyalty and trustworthiness are alien to a narcissist if their best interests clash with either value.

We all have narcissistic tendencies. As discussed before putting oneself first could prove useful in certain situations. It is the overdevelopment of this survival mechanism that becomes the problem in this winner takes all world. The narcissistic ego is purported to be the product of 21st century society and is partly the reason many philosophers see human beings as becoming more like machines. It is not too far a stretch on the imagination to visualize a cold emotionless human being separated from other humans emotionally but attached to their technology as an automaton. A robot like human when compared to the compassionate original that many feel no longer exists. Who needs those genuine human emotions when it is so much more secure to disguise oneself as human and stay protected emotionally. When one comes across a narcissist the emotions exhibited seem out of synchronisation and mis-placed. It can be very dis-concerting seeing someone pretend to be fully human for the first time. It as if they are performing carefully learned behaviours on cue and their timing and intensity can never be quite right. Reactions are just plain unnatural. However, only an authentic human being will ever spot this as being differently human.

> "The narcissistic orientation is one in which one experiences as real only that which exists within oneself, while the phenomena in the outside world have no reality in themselves, but are experienced only from the viewpoint of their being useful or dangerous to one. **The opposite pole to narcissism is objectivity; it is the faculty to see people and things as they are, objectively, and to be able to separate this objective picture from a picture which is formed by one's desires and fears."**
>
> **~ Erich Fromm - The Art of Loving**

I have lifted weights my entire life and have even entered some physique contests so I felt moved to comment on an accusation constantly levelled at bodybuilders as a group in many research papers, that they are narcissistic. I am assuming that to actually be a revelation, this must mean they are accused of being more narcissistic than most "normal" human beings. From my own point of view, having spent my life training my body, whilst having a healthy respect for my body and appearance and being very proud of my achievements in developing my 57-year-old body, I do not consider myself any more or less narcissistic than would be considered healthy in mainstream society. Remember that bodybuilding is a sport in which the body is the celebration, not scoring a goal or touchdown or exhibiting skill and abilities of the sport. Possibly the sport could be a reflection on society being more narcissistic than is considered normal. However, normal society is equal to bodybuilding when it comes to narcissism and I would agree that society in general may be more narcissistic than is healthy for the future of mankind.

I would say for myself that I celebrate my body conservatively, considering the work I have put into what I consider to be the ultimate challenge and an art form. Most bodybuilders, competitive or not, are modest enough. I am relatively introverted and as such competing was a massive challenge for me, coming after training for over 30 years. Whilst you do get the odd abnormally conceited individuals, I see more of those in an average day at university, the supermarket, or pubs and clubs than I have ever come across in the bodybuilding community. Most of the bodybuilders I know do not spend time on beauty products or hair products; they are interested in their project, which is their body, and it needs constant work. Normal behaviour is a full-body shave and often tanning, but this is usually only close to a show. I have seen extreme narcissism in bodybuilding so I suppose from that the sport does attract narcissistic types. Another case for not labelling but taking each person as they present to us in reality.

Posing is necessary and a sign of pride in their work. It generally would be performed reasonably privately, not in the street – that has more to do with self-respect, though. If you were a dancer, you wouldn't spend all your time dancing in public. Modesty would dictate different behaviour. I would say here that a top physique is a responsibility, and I would be the first to admit it can go to many young guys' heads at times. They may have changed, transformed virtually overnight from a body they are not happy with to a body that are ecstatic about. They want to show the world. Have you ever seen a woman who has just had plastic surgery not exhibit cleavage, or one with a new hairdo wearing a hat? There are numerous comparative situations in life. New cars, new clothes, and any physical change or perceived improvement will illicit pride from the owner – sometimes overly, because the change was deemed necessary. It was looked at as a need, maybe even thought to be the answer to a happy life. Why then is one more acceptable and considered normal and one not? Unfair? Yes, because it is the majority that ultimately decides what is normal.

We live in a society where being obese and lazy is acceptable but being fit and muscular is not. The majority rules, whether it is reasonable or not. As is often the case, I am glad I am in the minority; I feel it is a far more righteous place to live from. It's a place where fellow non-conformists are taking responsibility for what they do and not looking to blame or attack any other groups. Why? Because we are busy doing our thing, living our lives. To be honest, I would say that the attitude bodybuilders are accused of is more prevalent in those trainers with lesser bodies than with the more self-assured bodybuilders. A physique is something you need to get comfortable with, and that sometimes takes time. I would hazard a guess at this label having more to do with a lack of understanding of competitive bodybuilding than a real case of mass narcissism. Labels once again – my favourite subject!

Sartre once commented that hell is other people, I absolutely see what he meant. Where there are others, there is conflict. I am thinking that stereotypes and labels have far more to do with a total lack of understanding between different groups of people than any major reality issues. And yes, that includes academics. Maybe more than any other, they are charged with the responsibility of understanding. Are they up to the job? Maybe too much time is spent showing off academically rather than looking for any real truth. Any journal I have read, or academic I have spoken with – and I have yet to find any real exceptions, but I do live in hope – seem blinkered to the overall climate in favour of looking for any eccentric exceptions or behaviour that they can label and pass off as synonymous with the lifestyle choice of bodybuilding. This fits the falsely constructed stereotype that, for some reason, seems to suit others' emotional well-being. I will keep smiling through and think of myself as a goodwill ambassador for weight trainers and bodybuilders, although I refuse to accept responsibility for all of their behaviours. Bodybuilding is a variable project, different for every person, and should be accepted as such. There is no single object, "the bodybuilder". I am proud not to fit too well into any category. I am a square peg in a society full of round holes. I urge you all to join me. Maybe the sports choices of our young people reflect a general trend toward narcissism throughout society in reaction to the compulsive consumerism and emphasis on looks so prevalent in many cultures currently.

Narcissism is a major threat to society but should not be confused with the vanity that is rife in our society.

The Extreme Narcissist

People with Narcissistic Personality Disorders have an inflated sense of their own importance, a strong sense of entitlement, a deep need for admiration, yet a lack of empathy for others.

They use verbal abuse for power and control.

Narcissists need control and they like and love things that make them feel superior to and central to others. They want things to make them feel they are favoured, in charge, greatly admired and respected, or more important than others. Is that not common to many of us? At times and among different narcissists, these things (demands) may take any number or maybe even all of these forms:

- Power
- Admiration
- Sympathy
- Attention
- Prestige
- Money
- Popularity
- Pity
- Control
- Influence
- Status
- Service
- Praise
- Obedience
- Possessions
- Recognition
- Entitlement
- Righteousness
- Good Impressions
- Unquestioning Loyalty

These are expected as a birth right with no reciprocation or gratitude. As you can see this is a little more than vanity. Involvement with a person suffering from Narcissistic Personality Disorder or indeed living in a society with an increasing number of such people is a recipe for disaster. There is little hope of cure as

118

narcissists do not feel they need a cure as they are the centre of the universe. There are some great books available on NPD. If your curiosity is aroused, please explore it further.

Narcissist Check List

1. Two Faced, putting friends and family down behind their backs.
2. Tendency to blame their lack of success and failures on others.
3. Acts different in public than in private.
4. Irresponsible and unreliable
5. Arrogant, acts superior
6. Lives in a fantasy world which may include porn, flirting, affairs, and dreams of unlimited success and fame.
7. Addicted to fantasy oriented behavior.
8. Will lie and distort facts and change events to suit their own agenda.
9. Be irresponsible with money
10. Emotionally distant and unavailable unless they want something.
11. Lack sympathy for others, especially those they exploit.
12. Be very controlling and unable to relax.
13. Regularly provoke people and blame them for the fight.
14. Have trouble admitting their mistakes.

One final comment here is that the list above could be argued to be the ideal goals for the 21st century individual. Are we then creating a narcissistic society by teaching our young people that the above are values that will create the perfect life? This is indeed a worrying thought as we already have the seven deadly sins as the recipe for success. If this comes to pass and maybe it is too late, but if it does continue then authentic love will cease to exist if it hasn't already vanished from our consciousness. Do we live in a society where the seven deadly sins and the list above are already normal values for human beings? Quite possibly.

If you found the above list worrying, you are not alone and please remember we are all narcissistic to some degree and will see ourselves in these behaviours to some degree.

 Chatterbox Self

We all know what is like to be in a conversation and feel that what one has to say is so important that listening to the other person's chatter seems to be getting in the way. I remember reading that if you could see people's energy when they were in a conversation that most of the time it would be a battle to be the person with the most energy left at the finish of the communication. As the battle for supremacy leans one way then the other. Sapping the others energy and boosting one's own. We can all commit the error of believing we are the only ones with anything worthy to say. Never listening and only using the gaps in our speech to think of what to say next. Very often talking over the other person and interrupting them (pride). The enthusiasm and excitement of the exchange being too much for the restraint needed for a compassionate communication. We have heard enough about them now let's talk about ourselves. To talk about oneself a lot can also be a means of concealing oneself.

"My short-term goal is to bluff my way through this job interview. My long-term goal is to invent a time machine so I can come back and change everything I've said so far."

Could it be argued that if you want to create a good impression then a strategy of not speaking would best serve ones needs. We have heard the line that we have been given two ears and only one mouth so we can listen twice as much as we talk. The point being we need to listen more and that listening is where the art of conversation and communication begins.

Only a small percentage of what we say contributes to our communication, there is another 93% that goes on away from the chatter. That is wasted if we never know when to shut up or when to be in the present moment and become aware of all the subtle nuances that occur between two compassionate human beings. Any person serious about getting better needs to address their communication skills as a matter of priority.

> "Most people do not listen with the intent to understand; they listen with the intent to reply."

I have much to learn in this respect but I find that if I just think to myself that what I have to say is not really as important as making each other feel appreciated and valued. The connection is where the value is to be found in our meetings with others.

Spending more time silently communicating and listening to others is the place to start. This subject has been covered masterfully by Andrew Newberg, M.D., and Mark Robert Waldman in the book Words Can Change Your Brain. I would recommend this book to anyone looking to explore the rich subject of human communication in order to get better. I can think of others that leave me shell shocked when our turbulent interaction is complete. I breathe a sigh of relief and think how the communication was just plain hard work. I would describe these meetings as conversations between two egos. When one person awakes the ego in the other and the battle begins. Ironically for me and maybe you also this is the case with members of my own family. Ram Dass is quoted as saying that "if you think you are enlightened go and spend the weekend with your family." I understand that challenge completely and also understand that the challenge is inside of each of us as individuals capable of change and not in changing others to meet our communication demands.

It would be much easier to become enlightened in a controlled environment in your home or on the top of a mountain somewhere. But where is the challenge in that. It is not really possible to be one with all of mankind if you avoid them like the plague. That applies to all of life, so if you are selective in your likes and dislikes of animals, insects etc. that is not really in the spirit of spiritual growth either. I would say that whether you talk to all of life is entirely up to you but there is much study into the fact that plants are aware of your intentions and as such there is more consciousness around than one may have been led to believe to this point.

The word "listen" contains the same letters as the word "silent".

All of my plants have names and I can be caught regularly chatting away to all kinds of life. What is there to lose? They may not speak English but if there is genuine emotional intention behind your words they may be understanding you much better than you think. To be totally honest it is much easier to love plants and animals than it is some humans. It is a good place to practice and they rarely answer back or manipulate you to bait your ego. There have been times when Smudge and Jake my terriers have gotten me to react less than perfectly (anger). The way I see it if I can't react compassionately with two adorable small black dogs with the sole intention of getting food, fuss and walks, I have little chance of remaining Zen out amongst the ego dominated world that we all have to operate in. The art is to remain calm and in control at all times no matter what the provocation may be. Excuse me, I left the subject towards the end. However, it is all relevant to our progress.

 The Super-Social Self

Something like 93% of communication happens without words, with body language and by processes that we as yet do not fully understand. We are remarkable and complicated organisms and we know very little about ourselves. Are we heading in the wrong direction with communications away from developing our unique abilities in favour of handing over the task to impersonal machines and endangering losing our true human abilities, as surplus to requirement forever?

We all know somebody or we are that somebody that has literally hundreds of "friends" on various social media sites but never leaves the comfort of their front room without taking their contacts with them. Now! I understand that we are living in the golden age of communication but I for one believe that human beings are actually losing the ability to communicate face to face with others. When all of our so called friends are on our computer or we carry them with us on our phone when we go out into potential meeting new people situations, how can that ever be deemed social? I get fed up of saying good morning to people that have headphones or their phone stuck on their person and are oblivious and totally unaware of the world around them. Are we in danger of becoming more machine than human? No longer in control of the situation. Can we live without our phone? If the answer is an unhesitating no then we have a problem. I could understand a reaction of "well it might be difficult at times because certain important people expect me to be available but I could re-condition them to contact me at set times so I don't walk around constantly attached to my phone. So! Yes I could take my life back." I am afraid that the first answer is the dominant answer. We! My friends are owned by the phone companies. We have given much of our freedom away. Not to worry though because we will realize many other ways we have lost our freedom in the coming pages and we are not alone. I wonder how many dreadfully lonely people there are with long lists of friends on a computer yet not a real friend in the world. I decided here that social networking sites are places where you can quite readily witness all of the seven deadly sins within a very short space of time. Try for yourself. Greed, anger, pride, sloth, lust, gluttony and envy. There are some slightly different variations but these are commonly known. Sadly most of these are witnessed on social networking sites and actually seem to be revered behaviours in capitalist society. The seven deadly sins have become normal in today's society.

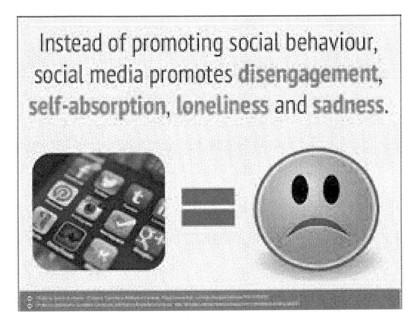

Is there a way to live in this world but not become a product of it?

Maybe having lived the answer to that question we will have lived a good life.

Smarty-Pants Self

With the availability of the worldwide web information has become a valuable resource and even the least bookish of people can seem to be well read. The problem with this is that the information has no value and is offered in isolated sound bites to make the know it all seem smart. The thoughts expressed are owned as personal opinions. They are then passed on out of context and with very little thought past the belief that it must be a fact and that elevates the smarty pants above you. Smarty pants rely on your being suitably impressed and not expanding the topic that they are masquerading as authorities on. The simplest form of the smarty pants is the weather forecaster. Rather than just accept the weather as it comes, accepting what is, we seem to need to know in advance and analyse each and every day according to whether we approve or disapprove of what we hear. In the UK we all seem to be very proud of our forecasting ability and are often very controlled by our weather conditions. This preoccupation with the weather succeeds in taking us away from the present moment and encourages wanting something less than what is (covetousness). Add to this the almost universal belief that there is good and bad weather and you can see why the discontent caused by many of the forecasts could be a real cause for concern. Tell yourself the story about how fantastic all of our weather conditions are and the world takes on a whole different perspective. I have been told that our weather conversations are more a check to see if the other is agreeable for an interaction before engaging in a more motivating conversation. That does make it much more understandable. Like dipping a toe in the water before diving right in.

Being right isn't nearly as important as knowing when to shut up.

Another favourite is the person that has acquired or swallowed a book of quotes and fires their wisdom at you constantly either in person or through the social media. The odd positive quote or advice about the weather can be very helpful to illustrate a point but not when taken as anything more than the product of shared knowledge through reading and only when appropriate. The fact that the original quote was not theirs never seems to feature in their thoughts. Possibly because they do not feel the need to have any original thoughts. Why think when others have done all the thinking for you. More often than not smarty pants are unaware of the background of their wisdom or the richness contained in the words they speak when used in the correct context. I am guilty of this at times and I have friends that base their whole personality on coming up with the right quote daily or proud that they got the weather forecast correct (I told you so – smugly) even though they repeated it straight off the television or radio report. That always makes me smile. We are all funny creatures at times. The worrying aspect of all of this is that we can all be sucked into this behaviour so easily. Becoming as sheep all following the lead of the others.

The smarty pants really come into their own when they are able to gazump everything that you say or have done or that you know. Gazumping is a word that came to light in the real estate industry. It is when a buyer offers more than the asking price to break into a deal that has already been struck. I believe in some areas there now has to be a signed agreement early in proceedings to limit gazumping. We all know somebody that gazumps everything that is said or done. Anything you can do I have done or can do better. Or that's enough talk about you let's talk about me. One of the smarty pants favourite haunts is pub quizzes or game shows on the television where they can use their extensive library of useless facts to amaze and astound those so easily impressed. I can think of one such television program appropriately called egg heads in which the 'stars' of the show not only give the answer but then take every opportunity to show off with extra useless facts. Having to be silenced as they sit with a smug look on their faces. A greater show of hubris (pride) I have never witnessed. The title of the show would indicate a slightly ridiculous side to this show that the contestants are far too thick skinned to feel the least bit embarrassed by. The responsibility of those with genuine intelligence is to use it to guide and help society and themselves, not to show off shamelessly for a teatime television audience with far too much time on their hands. I remember hearing once the sentence that if a person thinks they are enlightened then they most certainly are not. I would think that one could substitute the word intelligent for the word enlightened and be accurate. Intellectual potential is a personal potential for us all and whilst it can be used to motivate and encourage just the same as our physical potential, it should never be used to elevate oneself above any other person. Humility is the target here. We are all equally human.

Whether you are smart, fit or have a great body according to the ideals always use the gifts to help others realize their own perfection. I have a saying – And yes it is original or as original as words can ever be. **Getting better for me is holding the intention to be the perfect fit in the perfect universe and to help others realize they also are the perfect fit in the perfect universe wherever we are now.** You could call it my mission statement. It covers my behaviour standards and growth for myself and my aims of compassion for others and all of life. I feel it is a great philosophy to create a life purpose around and to help myself to keep growing by constant awareness of others. It is not as simple as it sounds as you will find out as you continue your journey through life with the aim of getting better. For me it is a zig zag journey towards getting better. As with all goals there is never a straight line to the goal. Constant reflection on the lessons life offers up is the only way forward. There are many highs and many lows to be contemplated but the path is always left open. The door to getting better never ever closes to anyone. The journey is easier if we all help one another to realise our potential.

> *"Its what you learn after you know it all that counts."*
> — John Wooden

The Spiritual / Religious Self

It is easy to think that if a person comes across as spiritual or religious that they have overcome the problems the rest of us have with the ego personalities dominating our lives. Think again. Where better for the ego to hide than behind the apparent solution to its destruction. Is the person that has a massive cross hanging around their neck on the outside of their clothing and that continuously quotes the bible in conversations really free from ego? I know that person and I can tell you the ego is more dominant then I have ever seen.

Take it a step further, how many religious leaders are actually worthy of the title and how many are playing a role that they feel frees them from the egos grasp when in actual fact they are merely play acting and hunting for power and prestige. Hidden in plain sight. Does an authentic spiritual or devoutly religious being need to parade themselves as such?

In my home town in the UK we have a guy that dresses in Buddhist garb and parades around in public juggling two balls in his hand. He is to be seen everywhere and I am afraid all I see is an ego that wants to be the centre of attention amongst people that dress in conventional clothing and go about their business in a much less obvious way. He may be a very fine human being but I am sure he has some way to go in awareness and acceptance of his ego behaviour to reach true spiritual enlightenment. I like to think that true enlightenment and love will not be so readily advertised and used to elevate one above others. There is another gentleman that walks around with a long staff, dressed in robes more suited to a time gone by and he can be found praying in the most unlikely places. I think the word I am looking for is inconspicuous, and he is not. It is my belief that a truly spiritual person will be conspicuous by their loving presence and not by their different clothing and odd behaviour. Odd, by the behaviour norms of the society they are living in. Both of these gents may be perfectly at home and normal in a different culture, a culture that follows these behaviours but here and now, all it does is say loudly, look at me. Many people in the past and present have, and are still, hiding behind a set of hypocritical values that do not ring true when all that they really stand for and celebrate is separation. Any group that celebrates themselves as good, against others as bad, will always fail when the unity of mankind is the only way the planet and mankind will be saved.

I do understand enthusiasm about a set of thoughts that one might like at any given moment but I feel that creating a physical manifestation of those thoughts is a little extreme and the thoughts then take on the power of an identity which then becomes more important than just liking thoughts and becomes part of that person's identity. This leads to narrow mindedness and an unwillingness to open one's mind to the constant change and evolution that our thoughts must be open to for our entire lives.

Science, religion and spirituality are progressing along a path that will forever change the way we think about our roles on this planet and the biggest challenge to that evolution are the narrow minded and dogmatic ideologies that many humans are clinging to as part of who they believe they are. There needs to be a – take what is working and move onwards and upwards attitude – or we will forever be stuck fighting the wars of the past over what are insignificant details that have grown over the years because people just won't let it go and move on. Any truly religious message has been lost amongst human pride, greed and power seeking individuals. Our ego fuelled friends above may seem harmless but on a much larger global scale the results are catastrophic. Religion means to re-bond or to re-connect. I don't see that happening. I just see separation. Religion is failing in its goal. Any 'us and them' attitude will forever bring the same miserable results that human history demonstrates so readily and the daily news reinforces on an hourly basis. When any human thinks they are better than another at the core of their being the result is invariably what you see in the news and all around you every day. Here the greatest sin is pride where there needs to be humility. Yes that is a challenge.

True religion is real living; living with all one's soul, with all one's goodness and righteousness.

quotespedia.info   Albert Einstein

Religion is best when it is not being talked about or labelled but rather obvious by the actions of compassionate human beings with all of life. There used to be a line used before children gained some empowerment that went like this –" children should be seen and not heard" – for me that is what religion should be about "religion should be seen and not heard". Stop talking about the good and just do it.

 Gadget Self – A Blind Alley to Happiness

I heard about a very good way of appraising whether a piece of technology has real value for the human race or whether it should never be allowed to exist. If the technology enhances the human organism it gets the thumbs up but otherwise it is useless or even destructive. There are many current technological staples that would fail that test. The problem may not be the technology but rather the overuse of it and the greed from the companies to bleed every last bit of profit from their product. The automobile may well go down in history as one of the primary factors in the destruction of planet earth. How many car owners' really need such a big car or need to use their cars as much as they do? But are too unwilling to change their lives, even for the sake of the future of the planet. I wonder at the sanity as I walk down the road of many cars per household parked all over the sidewalk/pavement so pedestrians have to walk in the road to pass. That used to be against the law but somehow it gets ignored by the authorities these days. As the profit from car sales is paramount to the greed of the 21st century. I see many Mothers having a rhino stopping truck to get their kids to school when it is just around the corner. We have no rhinos in this country and most of the offenders would benefit from the extra exercise out in the fresh air. There is not a person alive that would not benefit from more exercise.

Gadget self buys every gadget available at the expense of their humanity. More machine than human. Technology is great. The abuse of technology is a threat to our freedom and to the planet. It is a very fine line that most of the human race crosses without a thought to how it is changing who they are and how they evolve in future generations. These behaviours become the norm via mind viruses called memes and change the evolution of the human race. On the plus these memes can be positive also. We can make better choices and spread viruses that will save the planet or we can continue down the path of greed and more suffering and ultimately bleed this beautiful planet dry. Think about the technology that will really enhance your human potential and not what the greedy profit mongers tell you will bring you bliss. Bliss together with any human emotion worth feeling can only be found inside of yourself and that promise is a downright lie. Your purchase gives you a boost for a short time and then you are back looking for the next gadget that will really make you happy this time. How is that working out for you? They lie to you constantly. How do you feel about that? Still feel like lining their pockets? Buddhism makes it simple here – The secret is to want what you have and not want what you don't have.

I clearly see five of the seven deadly sins in gadget self. At a stretch I could include all of the sins but I don't clearly see anger or lust but the rest are all present and thought of as totally normal behaviour. Gadget self is normally covetous (craving), envious, gluttonous, prideful and prone to sloth. A lovely picture. A Frankenstein creation of the marketing man. One that he can sell to until his heart is content and his bank balance is bulging. Finally replacing him or her with the next generation of automaton, conformist consumers.

 Been There, Done That, Got The T Shirt Self

This is not the same as the "know it all" self as this self always admits to knowing nothing but always knows someone or a source that is an expert on absolutely everything. There is not one single topic of conversation you can broach that they will not hijack with either their expert version of what you are saying or any subject loosely related. I have one of these in my life and I never get the opportunity to speak for long. I even have to sit and listen to what someone on the bus says that overturns a thought that I may have inadvertently let pass through my mind and let slip out of my mouth.

Been there—done that. Then, been there several more times, because apparently I never learn.

There is normally a favourite "go to" source that reigns for a while. A person that has made an impression on this person. The reign is normally very short lived. The source can be anyone, the postman, a builder that has done work recently, the lady on the bus, the lady on the bus's son or an acquaintance, a magazine, a book, a newspaper, the television, the internet, any expert that is placed in front of this person is speaking the absolute truth. I am guessing that when away from me I become one of her experts to flout in front of others. Although I can't for the life of me actually remember getting the opportunity to impart any wisdom. I have learnt to sit quietly and just let her run on her own. She has little need for me in the conversation. This identity is ripe for social control. I am amazed how much capacity this woman has for filling her brain with details that are useless. The simplest point in a conversation can take an eternity to say. Something that can be imparted in seconds has to be prepared for meticulously and delivered with not one detail left to chance. I often have relatively important topics of conversation regarding family that are left unsaid while I listen to what I can only describe as hours of worthless rubbish. She then has the cheek to say that I don't tell her anything. It is impossible to tell her anything. As far as I can see she already knows every single thing that has ever occurred in the known world. I know I sound as if I must be exaggerating but if you know such a person you will know that this is real and one of the wonders of the world. A real test for any budding seekers spiritual growth. To make the point I have often said that I do not want to hear about certain people's turbulent lives in conversation (gossip) and even as I am saying that she can't shut up from talking about the very person I am fed up with hearing about.

YOU TALK SO MUCH SHIT

I DON'T KNOW WHETHER TO OFFER YOU A BREATH MINT OR TOILET PAPER

I hate gossip. The pain in her face when faced with having to not speak is a sight to behold. The scary thing is that we all have a little or lot of these identities in us all. I wish we all had the ability to see ourselves as others see us just for a fleeting moment. Psychologists would say the reason that certain types of identity grate on me is because I am looking at myself within the other. I am projecting my psyche onto others. I am actually seeing myself and I am not liking what I am seeing so I get rid of it on to another person. A case of "I don't want this trait, here you can have it". If that is the case! Ooer! I'm in trouble. I have noticed this before with other people and following a conscious effort on my part to discover why I am so bothered I have managed to deal with the issue in myself and the whole thing just disappears from my external life because I have dealt with it in the only place that I can, inside of myself. Isn't it fun to realise how we go about burying ourselves under layers of identity that we can't even recognise as the fake selves we have erroneously constructed to survive. We are a very complicated species. A worthy project for life. If we are honest with getting to know ourselves we should be able to see all of the selves I am writing about within our own psyches, either a little or a lot. Food for thought. I know I talk too much and it is on my list. My long list.

 ## Know Thyself

The reason we spend most of our time distracted with gadgets and rushing around is that we have a morbid fear of having to spend time alone with ourselves. Being quiet in a room alone with our thoughts is a situation that many humans avoid from the time they wake until the time they finally sleep again. The golden age of communication makes this easy. We never need be alone.

It is never easy to discipline oneself to work from home. This is something I have constantly been aware of and struggled with. At times I feel as if I am just keeping my head above water. I have managed, but should you ever take the opportunity to create from home, never make the mistake of thinking that it will be easy. It may well be the hardest adaptation I have ever had to make. Julie tried it once and lasted less than two weeks. Humans hate boredom; they do not like being alone constantly, and unless you are organised, you will fail. You will spend long hours doing nothing and failing to apply yourself. You will feel worthless and unproductive, and the mind games will begin. You will begin to question your whole existence.

This last few weeks I have noticed a disturbing change in many areas of my life. I now have to work too hard to discipline myself to walk the dogs, a job that I normally love. Reading is a chore, as is going to the gym. All of these would be top of my list of things I love to do. I have been a regular gym user for so many years and compete in bodybuilding shows. Now my reading is irregular and not at all concentrated. I am even deterred by the weather when planning walks. That is simply unheard of. I have begun to fall asleep when I am reading. I am constantly re-planning my workout and diet schedule in an attempt to re-motivate myself and make up for missed sessions and poor nutrition. To top it all off, I have not written a word for over a week. This behaviour is most unlike me.

This last week I periodically planned new starts in all of the above but seemed to fall at the first hurdle – not even a hurdle. All of the aforementioned are areas of comparative expertise for me. They are better accomplished without too much thought. Am I thinking too much? I am writing this by hand in the hope that the reflection might kick-start my more normal behaviour patterns. Some who know me might say that my current behaviour is more normal, and I am too disciplined generally, and I expect too much from myself. "Give yourself a break," they would say. They would probably encourage me to eat more junk food and be lazy more often. That is not who I am. For my life to work for me, I have to rely on self-discipline. It feels good. I must discipline myself to discover my seemingly effortless drive for the important areas of my life. The drive is anything but effortless. Looks can be deceiving.

As I handwrite this, the dogs are asleep next to me, having been walked by Julie alone this morning. The time for the gym has just passed. My laptop with current project screaming out for words is asleep, and my eating has been less good than usual. I sit thinking, which area attracts me the most to move my arse to change? I decide it is my writing, as I am already handwriting my journal. Surely it is only a few short steps from the couch to my desk. Where to start? It matters not, as long as I start somewhere. I have lists of topics. The first words are always the hardest to formulate. They need to come without conscious thought. Nothing comes. Am I afraid? Maybe, as I am nearly finished my book, and then my work will be available for others to judge.

I have always thought that if you search hard enough there is an opportunity to get better in every experience. Writing my journal informally whilst away from my desk is my re-discovered treasure in this instance. I have developed the habit of writing directly onto my laptop computer, and in the process I have neglected a very productive and therapeutic set of writer's tools. The rediscovered tools are a pen, paper, and the flexibility to write anywhere, in any mood, either with or without a lap.

It could be that, for me, sitting at a desk at an allotted time and ordering myself to think and reflect is the problem here. The position I am reclining in allows me to be part of my room, relaxing with Smudge and Jake, blue skies and birds visible from the window. The position allows me to look at my many plants and just take time to enjoy my surroundings between thoughts. It allows Smudge to lean against me, which she seems to love to do, I assume for security. Maybe I just needed a change.

I have come to the earth-shattering conclusion that both modes of writing are crucial to the process. A handwritten method can be used wherever I deem something worthy to be remembered and hopefully a lesson learned. And the work can be finished on my laptop, at which time even more reflection will have taken place (maybe) after the event, thus enhancing and expanding the thought for the finish.

Amazingly, once I began writing about a lack of motivation and discipline as an issue, I continued this piece and become aware of a total change in my attitude and motivation as I am writing. Julie says I am quirky. I have rediscovered an old friend, my journal. I am already planning events we will attend together. In the space of possibly 500 handwritten words, I have turned from pessimistic to exceedingly optimistic. Maybe Julie is right – that does seem particularly quirky. I had forgotten how much pleasure I get from writing my journal by hand anytime and anywhere. I recommend journal-writing to others constantly. When did I lose the habit?

It's a timely reminder and also a lesson on how easily one can lose certain habits that are so low cost and rewarding, yet capable of unlocking the door to your very soul if you can just allow yourself to cut loose. Journal-writing has always been so liberating for me. I care not who reads my journal. I have never really understood how protective some people can become about having their feelings shared. Your journal may well end up as the only place your authentic self can exist in our fake role-playing society of the twenty-first century. It may help you stay in touch with who you really are, if only for yourself. Keep a journal. It will be time well spent away from television and those exceedingly antisocial social networks.

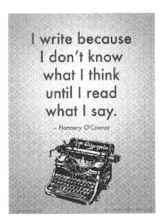

What about the other areas of my life? I had stopped being a writer at the gym or when out walking. I had stopped observing and reflecting. I had temporarily lost the curious part of myself that questions and analyses everything, the part that is never bored and always inquisitive. The part that sees a worthy tale in every walk, every encounter, and every gym session. The natural world, the unnatural world, and other people are all that I need as a writer. How strange that I lost my way with something that appears so naturally a part of me. Perplexing.

I will share two texts that I sent to Julie at this time, to give an idea of my struggle.

Text 1

> *Took the hounds. Back door open for them to bugger about. I needed the walk too. Very strange mood I am in. Creative Adam fighting to get out but mind too unfocused to produce anything but big ideas with little or no substance. I am sure this won't be permanent, and at least I am aware so I can fight and analyse it. It's not happening behind my back without my knowledge, and being gadget-free I have nowhere to hide. In my position of having to discipline myself, it does make life feel meaningless. I am achieving nothing. All I have is my training to conform to and any routine I can force upon myself. I have nowhere I have to be, no commitments except to myself. Maybe while I am like this I should get out with the dogs more often and train every day to give myself some structure. We saw Sunday the state of me if I stay in. All I did was sleep. A useless lump. Too much time and no motivation for anything. I need a relatively uncreative routine for this period. Just simple to follow without feeling redundant. Very strange, because I have so much I need to do but just can't get going.*

Julie's Reply

> *I can see you have been struggling big-time. X. Getting out with those two is always a good mood enhancer, bless them. X. The writing will always be there and come back to you. X. Easy for me to say. But you just have to ride it out. and eventually all will be perfect. X*

Text 2

> *Maybe getting to know myself that little bit better. I am sure I have taken the right path but had no clue how hard it would be to get on with myself. A challenge millions of people unconsciously choose to avoid their whole life. It would be more comfortable to conform and hide. Not now, though, because I know better and a tougher but more liveable life awaits. This feeling is part of the life struggle for an individual in our times. I had gone soft over the years, relying too much on distractions rather than face up to myself.*

What this thought has depicted is man's (not just me) struggle with freedom and an inability to be able to spend time alone quietly. Man conforms and distracts himself in order that he never has to confront his authentic human self. Jean-Paul Sartre stated that man was condemned to be free, and Erich Fromm highlighted man's fear of freedom in his book of the same name. What I experience are the symptoms and feelings that manifest as the inherent anxiety of a free man. Man is in a unique position of having separated from nature but as yet not having fully attained the destiny prescribed for the success of his own species. History should tell the tale of man's journey to his ultimate future, if he is to be a success. It's an ending that he may never reach, as it would appear man has lost sight of his destiny. Man's goals are widely accepted as being the total harmony between man and nature and between man and man. I think one could add between man and himself.

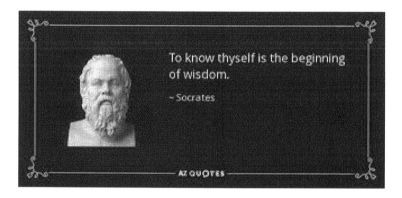

To know thyself is the beginning of wisdom.

~ Socrates

Maybe that is the place for each one of us as individuals to begin, by getting to know and becoming comfortable with ourselves minus technology and distractions and then using both sensibly to enhance human experience. Nobody said life was supposed to be easy. Get better. Wow! Isn't life complicate when you begin to look more carefully?

 Everything Changes

I think as a personal development author, one always believes albeit briefly that the next book will be the one that will define them. In reality defining an impermanent entity, such as the human psyche is impossible. One is changing a little or a lot every day, in fact every moment we are born anew in some way. My books are a snapshot taken on a pit stop at a particular period in my life. Nothing more. The desire, matched by the expectation is that my thoughts and experiences whether negative or positive will help others navigate their unique journey through life. Other authors, situations and life lessons have guided me, and continue to guide and light my way continuously if I remain awake enough to the lessons as they are revealed in many wondrous ways. Nothing is exempt from change. Everything changes.

 ## Be True to Yourself

Many individuals, and I use the term individual loosely to describe one of a herd, have formed themselves by trying to please others. Always feeling they have to do things because they are expected of them, or more important to make people like them, to be more popular. One can only hope that they finally say "to hell with it! From now on I am just going to be me – wealthy or destitute, good or bad, right or wrong, for better or worse. I have to do what I want to do; not what others feel I should do. It ends here and now." Sadly, many more never reach the moment of realisation and spend their whole lives inauthentically being for others as French existentialist philosopher Jean Paul Sartre observes.

Upon the realisation that they have been hiding their feelings from themselves and significant others, they no longer wish to be shaped and determined by parents, their culture or society norms. They do not want to form themselves and their behaviour into a form which is merely pleasing to others. They no longer choose to be anything which is fake, anything which is forced, or anything which is ordered or defined from outside of themselves.

What then can these individuals do that is positive after awakening to everything they do not want to be and have been up to now, what positive changes can be made?

They may choose the goals towards which they wish to move. Becoming responsible for themselves. They can decide what behaviour and actions have meaning for them, and what do not. They become self-directed and as such the authors of their own lives.

This freedom to be oneself is for many a terrifyingly responsible freedom that many choose not to face. There is a comfort in conformity. Individuals that move toward freedom move forward cautiously, fearfully and with little confidence at first. This freedom is a lonely freedom moving away from society norms and the comfort to be found in conformity. However, one of the basic longings of human existence is to be true to oneself, to have the psychological freedom that allows one to think for oneself, be self-sufficient, and feel whole and complete without the need for other groups or individuals to complete oneself. This first choice may be the hardest of all, but I can honestly say that once the choice is made to enter the process of becoming a new you every day through autonomous thinking and acting it is unlikely one will ever return to the brain numbing, living death that is the comfort to be found in conformity and psychic laziness. This is the only path to the personal and spiritual growth, which boils down to a search for meaning for living our lives which we as human beings yearn for so much.

 ## Values

Values are words and their deeper meanings that individuals and groups consider to be important and beneficial.

By expanding our values in both number and depth of meaning we can advance our characters from regression or being stuck in a rut to a progressive attitude and reality that brings joy to our lives as we transform in every moment. To make this happen we can examine our values and energise the words with emotions and deeper meaning. We can bring our values to life.

For most of the day our thoughts are negative as we have been subject to negative, limiting conditioning for most of our lives. However, by overwriting our negative programming we can change our thoughts and in doing so we can change our lives by choosing those thoughts that are unconsciously running our lives behind our backs.

We can also examine our negative thoughts and emotions that we do not value. Anxiety, depression, fear and anger whilst not stuff we value may have an even greater lesson to teach us than our positive values. And changing our attitudes to them makes each that much easier to accept. With a better understanding of them we can grow and develop through those lessons learned. In every moment there is a lesson.

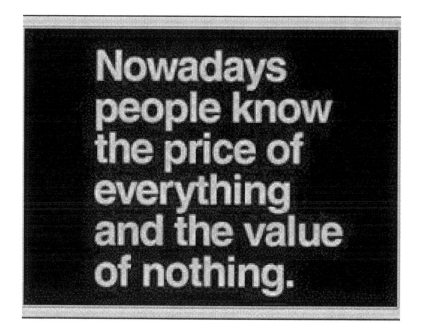

Unbeknown to ourselves we have all previously undergone significant conditioning by through our cultures, significant others, education, society and ruling classes. This "brain washing" is powerful and comes at us from the moment of our birth constantly from sources that we have learned to trust. Trusting these sources such as the media, religions, family and countless others has also been part of that conditioning. We are all involved in both sides conditioners and conditioned and have felt it is for the best. Maybe we have been wrong and it is time to reassess everything that we think and feel as normal. Wed behave the way we do because we are expected to behave that way, it is considered normal but is it in the interests of the human race for us all to be limited in such a way. We are docile and as such quite easy to control and our thoughts are not going to upset the status quo. There is very little original thought encouraged. George Orwell's thought police have been here for years and we just didn't recognise them. They are embedded in our education system and institutions as the right way. We have become blind to them. Their logic is our logic. There is comfort in conformity for our rulers particularly but how many of us feel that nagging anxiety for no apparent reason as if our souls require more and know that we are more than we are allowed to be.

It could be argued that we are programmed to live in fear (watch the news, I don't). We are definitely programmed for the profit of others and to be easy to control. We are relatively docile members of the "dangerous masses". The dangerous label has been used to indicate how dangerous we would be to our greedy oppressors if we ever realised our true powers and could be bothered about anything other than the storyline on the soap operas or where we will get the money for our next shiny toy.

Where does our freedom begin? By choosing the values we live our lives by we begin to become more free. By being aware that many of our values such as those below are being lived out we can then choose another way. Make no mistake these are all a big part of 21st century life on our planet.

The process of change can begin now. It needs to in order just to battle the continued mind manipulation that is happening to us all most of our days.

I will now move on to discuss the value of abundance and lead in to self-awareness that is the key to any changes we wish to make to ourselves.

Abundance

I have often wandered when self-help books urge us to affirm a life of abundance whether many of us are ready for the possibility of an abundance of darkness in our lives. It seems that as humans we experience opposites in reasonably balanced amounts. It could be argued that that "happiness" is only available once we have acknowledged the presence of guilt, grief, loss, betrayal, doubt, loneliness, depression, despair, obsessions, addictions, anger, fear, angst and anxiety as part of human existence and that those that appear to be happiest amongst us are those that learn to cope with the darker days in a more accepting realistic way. It is not a matter of being free from these dark forces of the psyche but rather being able to manage the darkness in alignment with the light in our lives.

Light cannot exist without darkness. It does help to understand that we all have equal possibilities for happiness amongst our peers and that even the seemingly happiest optimist will have to deal with the darker side of life. Just to lend to that optimistic view – the greatest lessons may be learned in the darkest moments. I know mine have been. It matters not if your material world is abundant. There are as many very rich depressed people as there are happy paupers once

153

immediate needs are catered for. Consumerism does not create happiness just a big pile of stuff and that familiar gnawing empty feeling inside that can only be temporarily relieved by more stuff before it returns again. All addictions and distractions end in the same way.

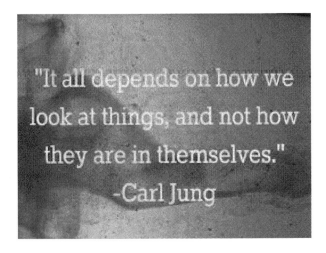

"It all depends on how we look at things, and not how they are in themselves."
-Carl Jung

We carry the seeds for light and darkness and contain all opposites in the same way. Wholeness or spiritual maturity is the managing of all that we are including a healthy ego to survive our cultures malevolent conditioning to become what we are meant to be. Our authentic selves. Our purpose in life is to get better. Simple!

Life is a balancing act between your true self awaiting release for better or worse and your cultural conditioning. The art being to be true to your authentic self once you are aware and can discover that part of your deeper psyche, and to be a valued member of your collective. However, the difficulty arises between your authentic self and cultural norms. The gap is huge and growing with every passing moment. There is no way your authentic Self can appear normal when normal values are so corrupt. There is some distance between the two. It is becoming increasingly difficult to marry the two, a choice has to be made between a comfortable conformist life and an authentic life. Being true to yourself. The latter makes the former impossible as examples throughout history have shown. There is a reason enlightened individuals live on the top of mountains alone. Sartre, possibly an introvert considered hell as other people but more importantly hell is 21st century cultures and it's potential for producing emotionless, narcissistic automatons.

So what do we want when we want a life of abundance? I would argue that most desire money, material possessions, sexual relationships, status and power. In fact, I would say abundance is really interpreted as getting a plentiful supply of all that is considered good in life and experiencing little or no lack in any way, shape or form. A greedy desire and a belief that this abundance will end any perceived suffering. We will of course share our plenty with others. How many people with enough stuff in their lives buy lottery tickets and why? Is more really going to be better? Gaining and affirming abundance then becomes less of a spiritual quest and more of the same shit attitude that has this planet in such a mess in the first place. I always think of the quest for abundance as the quest to have it all and yet be nothing. A quest that returns to go.

It doesn't have to be that way.

How can we value abundance positively? The one-line answer is to change the way we think about abundance. How? The first point we need to acknowledge how lucky we are and that all of us here in this moment are living in the land of plenty. We are blessed. We have a distorted view of what is needed to survive. Not having a television in every room and the latest trendy phone does not constitute poverty. The operative word being "needed". Once we realise that we are hooked and trading our freedom for lots of shiny stuff. We make a few people very rich and all powerful whilst our material world may improve our spiritual world collapses and we lose contact with who we are and what it means to develop as a human being.

If you are progressing spiritually and your material world is progressing also then you are indeed fortunate and have a good balance with very little greed and desire for more. This is of course if the progress towards wholeness is authentic and not just another mask to be worn, fooling self and others. We are indeed masters of illusion. Often we are the last to see who we really are.

If on the other hand you obviously crave abundance and lose yourself in the "more is better" and this is the default setting for most of 21st century society, you will never progress meaning in your life. Your big pile of stuff and or your yearning for more will never feed your soul with the meaning it desires. It is not possible to buy what your soul craves. Only upon this realisation can your journey into the second part of your life begin. The second part of life can begin at any time or never but is most common in midlife and begins with the realisation that life is not about who has the biggest pile of stuff or even being constantly in search of happiness. Life in the second part is in the name of meaning. The life quest is a quest for meaning.

I was thrown into the second part of my life as a result of extreme suffering about a decade ago (47), you can read much about this in my earlier books *Dazed and Confused* and *More Rebel Than Zen* which are book 1 and book 2 in the getting better series.

I love this part of my life and only wish I had woken up before. I meet others much younger than me that are starting to question their lives and as such are in transition and I envy that they have so much time to search for meaning in their lives. The first part of life is essential and can't be skipped. The first part of life is about developing the much maligned ego structures towards being strong enough to handle the meaning discovered in the second part of life. Our lives are constantly preparing us for what may come next. The first part is about being safe and secure and confident enough to survive all that is contained in part 2. Many get hopelessly stuck in part 1 and continue to inflate a protective ego, never feeling the call to self-realisation and wholeness. Forever clinging on to their world of stuff for fear of that being all there is. Missing the many messages our souls communicate to us via our mind-body. The angst and constant feeling that there must be more. Never stopping to care for the soul.

Part 1 of life is for ego development, and developing the strength and fortitude to survive. Survive what? This is in preparation for the second part of our lives. Part 2 of our lives entails an alignment of an already over inflated ego with our shadow and our soul. To over simplify - our egos must diminish, we must accept our shadow and care for our soul. Part 2 of our lives is an exciting exercise in getting to know our authentic Self. A quest that enthrals for the rest of our known existence and possibly longer. So many mysteries to reflect upon and so many more revealing themselves as the journey into the great unknown of our infinite inner space deepens.

As you can see our balanced definition of abundance is crucial to our life cycle and the addiction of consumerism backed up by television and media advertising (brainwashing) in general. This is probably the biggest obstacle we will face in attempting to find meaning in our lives and towards going some way to fulfilling our spiritual aspirations.

After getting rid of television from my life for many years, I have reintroduced it into my life but with a very selective choice of viewing but more importantly an awareness of what an enemy it can be when used without this acute awareness and in innocence by millions upon millions of unsuspecting viewers. I have named my television "Siren" as a reminder that it has the ability to lure me onto the rocks of mindless distraction and consumerism and it could be argued even to make one physically ill by selling disease through advertising suggestion. I believe this to be the case, that by using hypnotic suggestion our lives are shaped and controlled in a most devious way. I keep my set covered when not viewing and our viewing is very selective. It is my opinion that television advertising and promotions should be outlawed as it takes advantage of the trance states experienced during normal viewing to suggest without adequate or formal warnings of the dangers and influences that are possible. Billions of Human Beings watch television in blissful ignorance. That ignorance could be avoided. That is deceit. I often watch commercial sport with the sound turned down or record the programme and fast forward past the brainwashing segments. My favourite habit is to listen to binaural beat self-improvement downloads while I watch any programmes I favour. In this way I control my own brainwashing.

I avoid hypnotic commercial channels like the plague and as mentioned, I ensure I turn the sound down when possible. A note here - My Grandsons first words were "out now on dvd". Please do not value consumer ads or consumerism in any way. They are aware of what they do. The price of your soul's freedom is too high a price to pay for illusory abundance.

So there we have the value of abundance. How we as individuals define abundance as valued for our progress through the first and second parts of our lives or to fuel our greedy desires. There is always a choice. Knowing the difference between a need or something that is functional (enhances the human organism) and purely wanting more (greed) is becoming more difficult but if we are honest we can still see greed in much of the western world and in our own lives. Just because it is normal does not make it the right way to progress who we are. Normal becomes the enemy in the second part of life. The norms are distorted for profit, greed and social control.

It is clear that we can either regress or progress our psyche (soul) through the value abundance. We contain the possibility for both and just maybe our fate will be determined by acknowledging our distractions and addictions and working through them to arrive at an abundance that is just right.

 Addictions and Distractions

This leads nicely into discussing two values that I am guessing nobody would list as their core values but one would have to be blind and brain dead not to recognise the perceived value of any and all addictions and distractions in any culture. They must be considered valuable to take them into our lives in the first place. The aforementioned television and all that it offers is one of the biggest distractions on the planet if not the biggest. Often turning out to be the enemy that we have invited into our most personal space. Could our televisions be watching us as they were in Orwell's 1984? Our television – a value? The fact that it doesn't work out to be the case further down the line is unfortunate for the individuals but seems to be both fortunate and very profitable for somebody along the line. Let's recap a quick definition of values - Values are words and their deeper meanings that individuals and groups consider to be important and beneficial.

The habits that can be listed here are amongst the biggest business on the planet. We cannot imagine facing boredom, stress or problems without the use of caffeine, alcohol, nicotine, sugar, shopping, gambling, television, computer games, social networking, endless harmful gossip, overeating or drugs. The list is long and this is just the tip of the iceberg. Even while not considering ourselves addicted to many of these things we are all probably guilty of using one or more of the aforementioned as crutches to get through our days. I have always thought that a good gauge as to whether a habit is a problem or not is whether it can be considered to enhance the human organism and can it be "let go" with very little concern and withdrawal. We do not trust ourselves with our natural resources to survive unaided. What are we trying to escape from? In truth there is nothing that our mind-body cannot deal with, if we trust and get to know what we are. These are automatic instincts of our mind-body, endowments of our lively energy, in the course of life we gradually learn how to access and trust these instincts and use them with ease. However, these natural resources are not used or called upon, if, again and again, instead of accessing the power within ourselves, we substitute something external, alcohol or one of the many drugs both prescription and non-prescription that we turn to often urged by either well-meaning or totally indifferent experts. For instance, the totally natural ability to go to sleep is replaced by alcohol, a pill and subsequently we are unable to sleep because we have taken on board the suggestion that we need something in order to sleep. No surprise that by introducing such negative auto-suggestion into our lives we are right when we say we can't sleep. The pharmaceutical industry loves that outcome. The more of us that are on drugs the better for them and our rulers. In my life coaching practise I use hypnotic trances to illicit just that same auto-suggestion for personal progress. It is so simple just to stop suggesting negative outcomes to ourselves once we notice that we do it. Whether we suggest negative or positive outcomes we will be right. You can choose. I know what I choose.

I will call these addictions and distractions surrogate capacities. What do surrogate capacities do? They cover feelings and emotions that crop up in our lives. Feeling a little nervous? Time for a drink to cover up that valuable feeling. Thus numbing a vital part of what it is to be human. The alcohol changes what is going on and creates an unreal experience.

Surrogates, such as caffeine, alcohol, nicotine, marijuana etc., replace, blockade and ultimately extinguish our lively energy. We become split off from all the wonderful powers inside. The powers that are our lively energy. We are taking the chance of killing off natural lively energies and powers that ae possess. If each time we have an issue we turn to a substance, how can we ever learn to face anything. Obviously this takes in excessive television or internet, shopping, sex, gambling, drugs and much more. The task of mature adulthood is to trust our wonderful inner resources. Resources waiting to be found, activated and fully lived. I know that many will think I have just listed all of the fun stuff and that without those distractions life will be boring or unbearable. If that is where you are then that is where you begin.

> "All bad habits start slowly and gradually and before you know you have the habit, the habit has you."
> - Zig Ziglar

For most of these habits it is no longer within the realms of choice but has become automatic programming, conditioning that has been offered to us for others profit and our lifetime custom. We are not as free as we would like to think. Although appearing normal and that is the art of this control and programming, we are convinced it is either good or at the worst harmless to indulge and that we are making free choices. A master stroke by our two faced controllers. It is neither innocent nor are we in control, these habits make us docile and shut down our adult powers such as the power to question what goes on behind our backs. The ruling classes (whoever they may be) are made richer and totally in control of the sleeping masses (us).

Substances and habits are magical distractions that do not make anything consistently available but keep us coming back for more. Logically! Anything that keeps you coming back for more is something that can never satisfy you because even too much will not be enough. That is my experience with drugs and if any of you have experienced clubbing drugs you will know only too well the inclination to chase the high to excess. That is more or less the same with everything we are discussing here from shopping to gambling to eating to drugs. We need to re-evaluate and trust our own powers and resources, our own lively energy, an energy that moves through us and moves us. We can learn to accept and welcome our feelings by experiencing them lovingly without running for the hills or numbing our mind-body into a fearful stupor. Accepting and facing our fears is the fastest way to conquer them.

If by reading this section you feel alone in battling the fallen values of addiction and distraction, I would take a moment to point out that of all those mentioned I have been free of only gambling, marijuana and nicotine. Many are ongoing choices in my life such as consumerism and overeating but the awareness ensures I will get better at managing the onslaught and progress away from any and all dependencies in my life. I think I could say with some confidence that it is doubtful that anybody is completely clear of addictions and distractions in their lives in the 21st century as the intensity of the temptations increases and the onslaught is relentless throughout our lived lives. There is no escape but there can be an acceptance of the fact that the battle exists and it must be won for the sake of mankind. This awareness must include a knowing that the temptations will always be present and change disguises as the ruling classes need us to be hooked and hooked for ever and through generations into the future. Our oppressors need us to fail, to be numb, distracted and docile, never to reach our unlimited human potential or to be unaware of what might really be happening in our world. Not what they tell us but the truth. Wont it be good to prove them wrong and show that humanity can never be repressed. To be free from addictions and distractions and in touch with our mind-body and its total progress out of the limiting bubble they wish us to believe is all there is to human life. To evolve away from what we are now and what they expect us to be. We are much more. These first two values have led me nicely into possibly the most important value that we can possess as a core value, particularly considering the deceptions coming from our governments and institutions. Without the value of awareness our journey would be impossible and we would be exactly the docile and easily controlled citizens that the ruling classes need us to be.

Awareness is like the sun. When it shines on things, they are transformed.

~ Thich Nhat Hanh ~

OkyDay.com

Self Awareness

We hide behind our illusions. We are too afraid to question our conditioned, comfortable realities and perceptions because we are too afraid to upset the apple cart of a reality that allows us shiny stuff in order to comfort ourselves with delusion. We want to preserve our sense of certainty by maintaining illusions that we accept as the facts of our lives. Illusions at least promise that everything was ok, is ok and will be ok. This is why there are not more people in the business of self-awareness. However, there comes a time when shiny stuff and security is no longer worth losing our freedom for, there is a part of us that can't be fooled forever. We have a big pile of stuff and security but we are still not content as promised, there must be more. Rather than live with nagging doubts and intuitive feelings that up to this moment we have done our best to numb and ignore many of us begin to search for the real meaning of what it is to be human. We feel the power of the will to meaning in our lives. We enter the business of self-awareness instinctively knowing that the place to start is with ourselves.

"Self-awareness gives us ultimate human freedom"

Steven Covey

We begin to question everything and life gets more interesting than we could ever have imagined, even in our wildest dreams. Never did we realise we are so large and so capable and have been duped for so long. Our whole life becomes unstable, having been built on lies and deceit. With making the choice to become self-aware and the curiosity that creates we begin break free. Life is once again filled

166

with wonder and awe and we regain the appetite for living that had abandoned us somewhere along the way to gaining our security and amassing our big pile of stuff. Our moment is here now. We have been given a second chance. We all get multiple chances so just keep going and life will just get more and more interesting with the passing of time.

Awareness is a process with steps. We move from awareness, to mobilisation, to taking action that makes for change. More often than not we first become aware of our issues by seeing them in others before acceptance that they are also in us, this then amplifies our awareness and then change is possible.

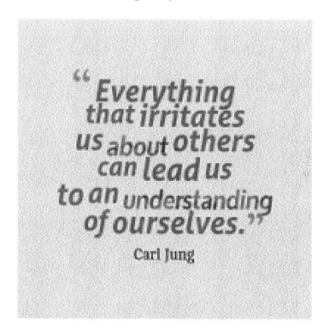

Whatever it is that irritates you in others is a good place to begin to know yourself. However, for many this never happens. Awareness

needs an admission of a problem and the desire to change the situation. This is just one form of self-awareness.

Awareness can also be awareness of our environment and of others. However, remaining true to the line "if you want to change the world begin with yourself" I will discuss self-awareness as being the springboard for becoming more aware across the whole of our lives.

Being socially aware is a matter of harmonising ones needs with those of the greater society. The positive, self-aware person will take responsibility for the consequences of her actions. She is conscious of the fact that her needs and choices do not exist in a vacuum, but exist in tandem with the needs and rights of others. The self-aware person works out a way of needs fulfilment that respects these rights and when she makes an error she atones for her transgression. This is something that is missing with Narcissistic personality disorder. For the narcissist their world does exist in a vacuum.

Human beings are not perfect. Ideals often seem perfect. More than we care to admit so much of our time is spent in a state of self-delusion. Often attempting to meet the illusory perfect ideals. Our internal chatterbox is busy justifying our actions, both good and bad. When we can't live up to these ideals and do something we consider wrong, our primal instincts kick in and we do anything in our power to avoid acknowledging what is often obvious to others. Sometimes it is all our fault. We seek external sources to shoulder the blame. Left unchanged over time, this behaviour becomes our routine reactionary behaviour and we become blind to it. We never stop to reflect on what we are doing or the consequences of our actions. We are unaware, and we are unaware that we are unaware.

Catching ourselves before we engage in our typical unconscious, default, programmed reactions is one of the greatest challenges of our lives, but when done relentlessly with discipline and moments of reflection we can change these conditioned thoughts, patterns and behaviours to new thoughts that serve us better and create greater self-awareness. This can be accelerated through using trance states such as hypnosis, self-hypnosis and creative visualisation. I use all of these within my life coaching practise to great effect. As mentioned before these techniques and trance states are also used against us when viewing the television and other mediums and once more to great effect by unscrupulous advertisers and oppressive governments that wish to control our minds.

There is a lot to take on-board for change to occur, one thing to be aware of is that our unconscious programming runs our lives with very little awareness for us and that is where we must begin if we wish to change our lives. If Not? We will keep repeating the same mistakes our entire lives. That is just not very smart. This can't be changed consciously as the unconscious is just too quick and has reacted behind our backs before we can react consciously.

Self-awareness is defined as conscious knowledge of oneself. I would add conscious knowledge of our unconscious powers to that definition. It is what we don't know that can hurt us. Self-knowledge about how our unconscious mind rules the roost. A fact that any manipulating power on the planet is all too ready and very able to use against us on a daily basis. This knowledge for us as individuals is a stepping stone to reinventing oneself and casting off the chains of any conditioning not serving us well to this point. We can then learn to make wiser decisions and it helps us tune into our thoughts and feelings, developing our previously neglected intuitive powers.

So often we blame something or someone outside of ourselves because it's the easiest excuse to find a scapegoat for our issues. When we do this we give away our power to progress from the situation. We must empower ourselves by thinking about our misguided thoughts and beliefs, reflecting, trying different perspectives and learning and changing from our mistakes. This in not always the instant solution that we seem to demand in the 21st century but the tension held in the situation will produce a choice that feels right.

As we develop self-awareness we are able to change our thoughts, a process that is made easier by using the trance techniques mentioned previously to communicate with our unconscious at the level of awareness at which it operates. Changing thoughts and interpretations in the mind allows us to change our emotions. Success arises when our conscious beliefs are in alignment with our unconscious (great) expectations. Expectations that we are completely unaware of, unless we have done the work to programme our unconscious ourselves. An example is with affirmations and why people get such differing results and wildly conflicting opinions on whether or not they work. Affirmations are quite simply consciously stated words unless they can become imprinted on our unconscious with emotion and feeling and become a part of our autopilot behaviour, become expectations. I do believe this is possible consciously with repetition, passionate dedication and an unwavering belief in the process. I know it is quicker and more probable in trance or drowsy states.

> # Any idea, plan, or purpose may be placed in the mind through repetition of THOUGHT.
>
> Napoleon Hill
>
> WWW.VERYBESTQUOTES.COM

The dedication required to explore our inner space and change our mind and behaviour is a challenge particularly as the actual process is a new behaviour and as such will improve with practise. There is often an inner resistance at the beginning even with the most resolute among us. It is within human nature to create routine and habits. Automatic behaviour triggered from our unconscious mind requires that our brain exerts less effort and uses less energy. How much easier is driving once we become experienced and it becomes a unconscious behaviour compared to how fatigued we get when concentrating on learning the process. It does require discipline.

The problem before we become aware that we even need to be aware is that we are vulnerable to outside influences from significant others, the media and countless other sources both well-meaning and not so well-meaning. The danger in this is that we are being run by others ideologies believing them to be our own and we get comfortable doing things against our true nature that it becomes difficult to know what our authentic nature is. We believe that this inauthentic impostor that has been created by ourselves and many others is really who we are. Once (if) we begin to open up to awareness we are better prepared to protect ourselves from such influences, such as television advertising and the propaganda portrayed in what passes for news when in all probability it is more fiction than truth. A good starting point would be not to believe a word or turn it off.

Eventually awareness causes us to question many of our "normal" behaviours and we start to see them as robotic and conformist. We see our thoughts opinions as not our own and merely a product of what can reasonably be called brainwashing for control and profit. We have chosen our thoughts and opinions from what our oppressors made available and that is far from a comprehensive list in any situation. We have been cleverly convinced that we are free when in reality we are automatons reacting to our limited lives just as predicted. We are living Orwell's 1984 and Huxley's Brave New World and have been for decades. There are many more messages from writers and film makers depicting our real plight that we are just too naïve to see the similarities in our lives. The thing to keep in mind is that these stories come from the psyches of human beings just like us and I for one find more truth in fiction than the truth that is being fed to our living rooms and gadgets for us to live our lives by. I repeat this quote by Aldous Huxley –

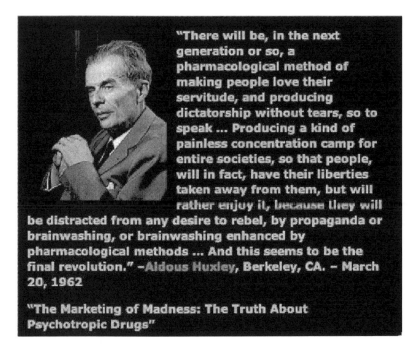

"There will be, in the next generation or so, a pharmacological method of making people love their servitude, and producing dictatorship without tears, so to speak ... Producing a kind of painless concentration camp for entire societies, so that people, will in fact, have their liberties taken away from them, but will rather enjoy it, because they will be distracted from any desire to rebel, by propaganda or brainwashing, or brainwashing enhanced by pharmacological methods ... And this seems to be the final revolution." –Aldous Huxley, Berkeley, CA. – March 20, 1962

"The Marketing of Madness: The Truth About Psychotropic Drugs"

Self-awareness is a choice. When a bright light shines on our flaws, do we embrace ignorance as being bliss? This is the stance of the majority or even worse making out that we are well informed when all of our information comes to us from less than trustworthy but tremendously convenient sources. All we need to do is keep an open mind all of the time and be willing to have our beliefs change as we indulge our curious natures in the search for meaning. Do we escape the reality of who we are and drift along with the rest, making the same choices because it is comfortable, convenient and doesn't rock the boat? Or do we face ourselves, accepting and aligning our soul, shadow and ego and moving progressively on a path that allows us to rediscover our authentic selves beneath the fake conditioning, to embrace our best, truest selves, regardless of how lonely and painful it may be at times? Progress here is toward

174

becoming authentic. Awareness leads to progress and getting better only if we resign ourselves to work at it. To no longer let those who have fallen into a comfortable, normal, conformist groove tell us that this is how life is supposed to be lived.

To act upon self-awareness means differentiating ourselves from the tribe and thus making us vulnerable to being rejected, excluded and all of the other fears that authentic self-awareness and action will illicit. As with any fear the cure is to go through it.

To be conscious of who you are, how you think and what you do is invaluable because it leads to self-knowledge (knowing thyself). Knowing that the process is fluid and ever changing means that change is a certainty in all of our lives, so we might as well choose our own changes and not get swept along with the herd. To be conscious and mindful of our fears, thoughts and behaviours. Developing the courage to own the right to be different and using the awareness to progress. Getting better in all aspects of your life according to your authentic self. Distancing ourselves from the powers that wish us to be the same as everybody else is wise until we get strong enough to resist the paltry temptations intended to keep us firmly attached to the herd.

We must learn to face ourselves, to admit our mistakes, to learn from them and to let that awareness motivate and change us. This is taking responsibility for the quality of our lives and for our constant progress. We can get better in every way on a day to day basis. There will be hard times but overall the progress will be constant. The greatest leaps forward come from the darkest moments and the lessons learned about ourselves and others. We must also learn to be loving, patient and compassionate with ourselves because change is a process and comes slow and steady. Overriding existing programming and creating new habits that suit us better will define who we are and signpost our progress.

We must realise that this process of discovering ourselves is difficult because everything from cultural influences to our reptilian brain is fighting against our being free from automaton status. Our own unconscious mind will feel like the enemy often, making us behave in ways that are automatic but no longer what we want consciously. The new behaviours must be made unconscious and become our automatic responses. The fact is our unconscious has acted and will always act before we are consciously aware. It is just quicker. It would be much easier to conform, throw tantrums, blame external sources, offer readymade excuses and to flee from the painful reality of owning our flaws and mistakes. The progressive process of striving to get better, our heroes journey is rife with hardships and obstacles but is an amazing way to spend the second part of our lives. Nothing worth doing is ever easy. An examined life is the only life worth living.

As we become more self-aware we no longer include others as the cause of our pain (parent, society). We no longer look to remove ourselves from the pain, we simply roll with it and let it pass by. Awareness befriends pain, harvesting the lessons, rather than dodging or repressing it. The inclusion of our parents and other outsiders as the culprits that made us so inadequate loses its meaning. Leaving no blame, only answerability that may or may not ever be acknowledged by them. In my experience 'not'. We are aware of our past and grieve it, we honour our past but are now more passionately involved in the present moments and with things that we can affect for ourselves. At this point when we no longer fight shoulds and we have released resentments, life gets easier. We have learned to let go. We lose inhibitions and transform anger at those we blamed for our inhibitions. Acknowledging that they did the best they could with what they knew at the time.

This doesn't mean we have reached a "fixed climax" of awareness but that we are progressing and our awareness is removing obstacles that we were stuck against, allowing us to get better. We are maturing with our awareness and may still become the person we always wanted to be. The process continues for life and the ripple effect our loving energy has on others becomes our legacy.

 Creating Great Expectations

We, as humans are in the process of being enslaved by malevolent forces. These forces have been and are continuing to be written about by others and the reaction is indifferent at best. I will leave a paper trail for you in the books of interest section that I include at the end of my books. Please explore it at your leisure and your personal world view will take shape accordingly. This exploration in itself can be an amazing experience. Beginning to understand what may be going on behind our backs. I would say this type of study is vital to developing a well-rounded world view away from the one we are being fed by our oppressors. This has been happening since our birth and our whole life system is part of this process of enslavement.

These forces require that we remain docile and living in constant fear. We are governed by powers that are not in our best interests. We are lied to, programmed and mind controlled so that we come to firmly believe that we are free and our thoughts are our own. This happens until such time as we individually and collectively wake up to our own powers that will ensure our freedom and evolution and the failure of our largely "invisible in plain sight" oppressors to enslave the human race. Our oppressors expect us to conform and will lead us into enslavement. They will continue to fabricate a world in which we need them to protect us in order to show a fake nurturing face to the world. And win our favour and loyalty. They do not deserve it and much that we fear in the world is created by them so that they may then save us from the bogeyman. We are brainwashed our entire lives and under constant mind programming drugs and techniques. We believe this is normal and we are indeed lucky to live under the wing of such caring rulers. Our expectations are low and because of this we are limited in what we can become by our state of minds.

It is under the influence of our programming that our expectations are so low and that we limit ourselves to what is considered normal. We suffer needlessly. We are tampered with at every turn. We are drugged, offered shiny toys, distracted by bright lights and fantasies and turned into little more than docile robots. We often drug ourselves into a useless stupor with "legalised" drugs such as alcohol and soon to be marijuana. These drugs render us as harmless and controllable. The war on drugs? Don't make me laugh. Our rulers are the biggest drug pushers on the planet both legally and illegally. They control the drug use on this planet. They have no intention of ever having a drug free society. Even our children are prescribed drugs as soon as is possible to get them used to drugs as the normal behaviour of human beings. The syndromes are invented and the drugs prescribed for profit and social control. Every day in every way we are diminished more and more by our oppressors, masquerading as benevolent rulers in a system moving towards total enslavement of humanity at a remarkable rate. Each new war, technological breakthrough or law change brings us closer to doom. We live grinning with our shiny new toys, new legal and illegal drugs and mindless distractions. All will cost the future of the human race. We have low expectations as we are not yet awake enough to realise that all is possible for the human mind and even great expectations may be easily realised. Our limitations are our imaginations.

> The most important thing in life
> is to stop saying "I wish"
> and start saying "I will."
> Consider nothing impossible,
> then treat possibilities
> as probabilities.
> *Charles Dickens*
> David Copperfield

How can we fight mind programming?

By taking responsibility for our own minds just the way we would accept responsibility for our bodies. We can re-programme our minds for ourselves. We have the ability to control our own minds. We can rediscover exactly what it may mean to be human.

What are our capabilities?

Who are we?

We first need to wake up to the enemy within our midst and neutralise their effect on our minds. We can then and only then remove them from our reality by awareness – progress and just plainly getting better. We can rise above such domination to a place where they can no longer reach us.

This begins by becoming our authentic selves. Ignoring what we are told and sold as normal and striving to discover the unique individuals we all are once the limiting programming and mindless distractions are left behind. We need to focus on becoming more than we are. Forgetting or questioning all that we have believed is fact to this point is a good start. Not believing what we are told in the news and anywhere else that information comes to us so readily is also wise. Think about it! What is the first thing to control when war breaks out? Information. Propaganda. Don't be so ready to think we will not be lied to. And maybe we will never know the truth. Mistrust all sources of convenient information that come free and often. Our oppressors own every one. Question every rule and the more it seems good for the community the more we must hunt for the hidden agenda.

Total self-mastery which is our goal, means personal and collective power, means understanding, means love, means happiness and what it is to be in control of our health. The goal of our lives is towards meaning and understanding as much as we can know from birth until physical death or transition away from this reality. That depends on your world view as to how limited is our consciousness and does it live on or not. One of the many mysteries of life that we will have to include in our world views as it changes and evolves with our development.

We live by suggestion and auto-suggestion. We are governed by our unconscious minds. I like to call the unconscious mind our true soul mate but too us at this point it is s stranger, acting in ways that we do not understand and making us behave in ways that we do not intend consciously. It rules our lives and has been and continues to be programmed by malevolent forces that understand our powers better than we do – for the enslavement of humanity.

This is not all doom and gloom once we wake up and start to notice what may be happening behind our backs, we can happily and with purpose guide our own development and limit our exposure to damaging entities by creating a world different than the norm for ourselves. However, like anything worthwhile effort is needed, auto-suggestion has to be learned and accepted. It is a matter of educating ourselves up to the point when better control of our own unconscious is attained and then getting better into an unknown inner space with potential as yet unrealised by any human being. But I can guarantee our oppressors are far advanced in this and motivated by the need to control us. Our goal is to get better and learn to control our minds with no limiting expectation other than constant improvement. Self-mastery of our mind-body and discovery of our authentic selves through examining our lives with a passion for transcendence of all that has come before.

In my Soul2Whole Life-Coaching business I work to progress my partners to become self-reliant. We re-programme negativity with chosen thoughts and learn to know the threats that become very obvious and so protect ourselves from further brainwashing. I teach partners via trance states, cognitive reasoning to have the greatest expectations possible and the drive to transcend any limiting beliefs using the same suggestion techniques that took away our freedom up to this point. My partners then move on to influence others through the ripple technique, leaving a priceless legacy long after we no longer need the gift of our fantastic bodies.

Having great expectations means we must no longer think normal. Normal is what will enslave us. Once our unconscious mind begins to live up to that soul mate tag and is operating with ever greater expectations and knowing that we have as yet unknown potential without question we will rise to freedom. What appear as miracles and magic in our current reality will become our new expectations.

Progressing through our life process having neutralised our oppressors will be the legacy we leave our future generations so that they may then transcend us once more. Our life purpose has always been to transcend those that have become before.

This power is possessed by each of us. Others such as myself for you can help you discover your latent talents but make no mistake the power is within each of us. The first step is acknowledging this fact in such a way that the belief becomes imprinted on our unconscious mind. Once we have that faith in ourselves and our natural talents, the progress will follow. We will have removed one of the biggest barriers to progress, placed in our psyches by our oppressors over the years before awakening. The belief that we are limited. We are not limited, except only by our own thoughts. Everything is possible but we have to believe it is possible for us deep inside our unconscious minds. Believe what you want to achieve, read, learn and observe until you know this is the truth. Progress will follow when you have made the unbelievable believable for yourself at a deep level. Dare to imagine what now seem like miracles and with 100% faith and a deep expectation these miracles can become the norm and your expectations will become even greater. This has been programmed out of us and we are bombarded with negative energy daily via our gadgets to keep it that way. In my book **Getting Better Series Book 4** - **Sometimes I Pretend I am Normal** I discuss some ways that I personally create in my world to protect from malevolent forces and create a sanctuary for myself and Julie, my wife.

 Our Mysterious Minds

If I asked you - where are our minds? A vast majority of readers would probably point to the head. Mind (consciousness) is separate and apart from the physical organ called the brain. It is possibly best explained as being everywhere (energy) with us being receivers. Similar to a computer receiving the internet. We could be argued to be as organic computers and the mind is cosmic consciousness. There are numerous theories as to the existence of a pervasive field of energy with such names as Cosmic consciousness,

God, the Zero-point field and the Morphic field being given to such a phenomenon. There is little doubt that this field exists, whatever it may eventually be named. It would be amusing if it weren't so tragic that human beings seem to love arguing, fussing and fighting over details when it is obvious from the outside that they are arguing over the same thing. We have made very little progress in that direction in the entire time humanity has existed. So advanced in so many ways and yet so backward in others. It is like giving children the most advanced and dangerous weapons to play with when we are charged with the responsibility to use our technology responsibly. From mobile phones to nuclear weapons it is always inevitable that humans will abuse the privilege of material progress with an obsession verging on insane.

Back on the subject of the unconscious mind, we are seemingly limited in our ability to receive by obstacles and barriers that could be compared to firewalls. These have been put into place and are maintained by our malevolent ruling entities in order to enslave the human race to do its bidding. We can access our own minds using similar methods for our development as are used against us for evil and to free ourselves from this tyranny.

Knowledge is power and in this case knowing how to begin to master our own minds by understanding how they work is our road to empowering ourselves and ultimately more freedom.

We are blessed with one of nature's greatest gifts in the relationship between our minds and bodies and yet many of us still view them as separate. We know so little about the mind-body connection. Awareness and curiosity are the keys to begin unlocking the mysteries of the mind and to free ourselves by discovering just what we are capable of. Thus freeing us from the daily brainwashing in our lives towards transcending what we are in every precious moment. We have become docile and too easily pleased with a material world of ever increasing piles of meaningless stuff. The time is here and now to understand and use our own minds intelligently and to our own best advantage to break free of the human control behaviours that have become the limiting and enslaving norms for mankind. We need to develop what it means to be human and to use our sleeping human abilities to further the development of the human race. Beware of all that becomes normal social behaviour. There is always a hidden agenda favouring our oppressors.

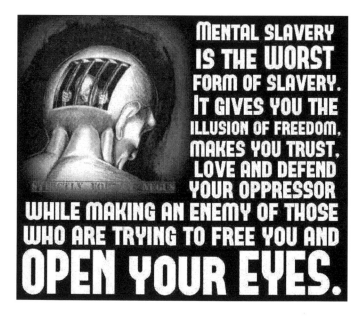

I want to give an example of what I was just discussing, the legalisation of marijuana. Marijuana is a firmly established human habit, albeit illegally. However, lately the stories of this miraculous drug have been intensifying to the point of it seeming to be the remedy for everything that ails us. That is just a teeny bit coincidental as the case for worldwide legalisation looms. Remember who really controls what we read and think! The spin doctors of our evil oppressors. So now marijuana will become the "norm" right there with alcohol and any number of prescription and legal drugs. Generations will grow up with it as an option to make them feel temporarily good and to deal with the boredom of life. This will further ensure a docile society that choose to numb this fake reality in order to make it bearable (they think), rather than break free into the limitless reality that is ours by right. The masses, from what I see on social networking sites seem to believe this to be a victory. Legalisation would not happen if it did not tip the balance in favour of our malevolent controllers. A rookie error made possible by the short sighted masses being interested more in hedonistic pleasures than transcending this reality. Another shiny distraction.

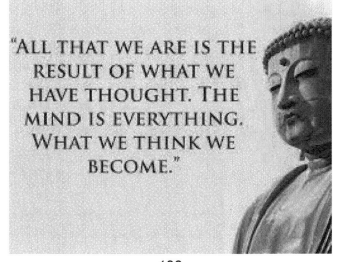

This choice being made now is choosing for countless millions in future generations that will have to deal with an even more drugged up reality in order to transcend former generations. Are we condemning our future generations to a life of docile obedience? I sincerely hope that we are not condemning them to a life in chains due to our own short sighted selfishness and naivety.

Our amazing mind can be best understood by viewing it as a single entity in three parts, the conscious, the subconscious and the unconscious, ranging in depth from us being totally aware of our conscious mind to being gradually less and less aware until we are oblivious to what our unconscious minds may contain. The problem here is that contrary to the belief of what we don't know can't hurt, in fact what is buried in the depths of our minds can create a life of misery and despair. In reality, what we don't know can and is hurting us more than anything else because we are often helpless against our own minds. This results in behaviours and reactions that we have little choice in affecting. The task for us then could be to reunite our mind's parts into a more cohesive unit toward understanding and reconnecting with our mind in its totality. To begin with, this entails becoming more self-aware by studying ourselves according to theories on personality and our psyches. Knowing ourselves better. The beauty of this undertaking is that as yet nobody knows or understands fully the capabilities of the human mind and the connection to universal entities such as cosmic consciousness, the Morphic field, the zero point fields and a very workable concept of what might be called God. I suspect science and religion are only far apart on pig headedness and that all arguments are over power and reduced to petty details of the same phenomena which quite frankly nobody fully understands or is able to explain and maybe never will. It is worth remembering that many of quantum physics findings are as supernatural to our current beliefs as are religious miracles. It would seem that any belief system has the effect of stopping us learning the truth by narrowing our minds. Our tasks maybe to learn to open our minds fully to anything however impossible our limited world views may make it seem. Remembering that we have been programmed to stunt our development, to enslave us to others will, so what we think we know is holding us back. We know nothing. Be wary of opinions and be ready to change your mind frequently in order to develop. By all means have thoughts that you like at this time but never make them your opinions as we hold on too tightly to our opinions when they have long since lost their usefulness. Mind is a process of continuing change and discovery. A place where doubt can be your best friend and keep your mind wide open to other possibilities.

The conscious mind can handle the least amount of information for processing (5-9 bits).

The conscious mind is our awareness at the present moment, such limited processing capabilities only allow for simple tasks. Mindfulness is the art of being conscious in the now of daily tasks. This proves difficult due to the amount of time we are controlled by the unconscious and unconscious parts of our minds.

> "Whatever we plant in our subconscious mind and nourish with repetition and emotion will one day become a reality."
>
> Earl Nightingale

The unconscious mind consists of accessible information and has unlimited capacity. We become aware of this information once we direct our attention to it. A good example would be the skill of driving a car. Our conscious mind is not able to process all of the information needed to drive proficiently from the outset and so learning to drive is a matter of the information becoming imprinted on the unconscious via repetition thus allowing driving to move from conscious learning to both conscious and unconscious and eventually to becoming a unconscious behaviour that we do not have to be aware of or think about consciously. This leaves our conscious mind free to attend to new situations presented to us. Teamwork. Talking whilst driving is an example of a conscious act performed while we are driving unconsciously. How quick the talking stops if we are called to action to attend a situation not previously learned. A dog in the road or such like will need all 5-9 bits of our information processing quota for our full conscious attention. We can see here that multitasking is something that comes down to information processing and our unconsciously learned behaviours and nothing more, particularly not gender as erroneously believed.

Repetition
Repetition
Repetition

The unconscious mind (deep) consists of primitive instinctual drives as well as information not so readily available or brought to consciousness. Our unconscious can be seen in our behaviours that seem uncontrollable. From inside of the womb onwards we acquire countless memories and experiences many unpleasant that have formed who we are today. However, we cannot easily recall most of these deep memories. They are our unconscious forces often called our shadow that drive our behaviours. Our task towards progressing through life to adult maturity, if we decide to take it on, is to align our mind – conscious – unconscious and unconscious to work well for us in our life situations. I was going to say to align in perfect harmony but I am not sure we need perfect harmony but rather the ability to transcend what we are to this point and to transcend what it is to be human to this point. Simply! To get better. A much more achievable goal and one that our minds will believe and expect. Without our minds blessing with our goals we will get nowhere. Call it faith, belief, expectations or whatever, we have to believe and expect what we intend at the deepest level for our world to change. This is why the law of attraction works for some and not others because at that level of unconscious mind our intentions contradict our conscious intentions. We can't know our unconscious intentions but we can work to change them to be more in line with what we consciously expect or intend. To put it simply our conscious mind has to be able to convince our unconscious minds that the intended is both possible and the best for us. Quite a challenge when we have no clue as to what is driving our unconscious mind or to what programmes it is reacting.

Our minds contain everything and accepting this fact is a good start, all opposites are within our mind. Allowing all parts of our mind to exist as one rather than fighting to eliminate one half of an opposite is wise. winning/losing, eating/fasting, action/passivity, good/bad, earning/giving, sex/celibacy and the list goes on, accepting both are within us leads to a healthy mind, a good place to start rather than making a stance on one side against the other. This helps us to lovingly accept our own shadows which we will have to live with if we ever hope to get better and move past our limiting programmes. There is much to be learned from taking the middle ground, there is an area that is just right and when we very occasionally spend time in this zone we know we are close to achieving the ultimate state of mind. The balancing of all of our opposites can only ever be fleeting but nevertheless is a worthy goal for life.

The Power of Suggestion

Give a batch of brownies to someone who's never had pot before and tell them they have pot in them.

Watch them act high.

Laugh.

By working with our minds through meditation, hypnotherapy, Eco therapy, bibliotherapy, creative visualisations, dream work, heartfelt affirmations and generally becoming more aware and communicative with our unconscious and unconscious minds. we can build a programme for getting better at being human and move towards developing not only ourselves but changing what it means to be an average human being.

Repetition is a vital component and you will find in my written work many cases of my repeating points very often, this is both for myself and for my readers. I know that personally I have read the same thing many times in the past before finally knowing it. Repetition is used against us endlessly throughout the day, think of the ever repeating ads and media crap that we are soaking up constantly I whatever hi-tech gadget that we use and think about how we have made those suggestions part of our lives. It works against us so why not choose to use it for the good of your mind.

I want to give an example that you will all recognise as communication with your unconscious. At the drowsy point of falling asleep we are in a trance state (hypnogogic), this is a great time to talk to your unconscious and you have all done it more than once.

How often have you wanted to wake up at a certain time and have managed to do it without an alarm clock? There will be other instance in normal waking time when you have thought about something, maybe an intention to be somewhere at a certain time and then having let it go (forgotten about it) arrive exactly where you wanted to be or exactly where you told your soul mate (unconscious) you would like to be. I call my unconscious my soulmate as it can either be your soulmate or your greatest enemy, that is your choice.

Meditation, hypnotherapy, Eco therapy, bibliotherapy, creative visualisations, dream work, heartfelt affirmations and generally becoming more aware and communicative with our unconscious and unconscious minds allows us to overwrite many of our negative programmes and improve our self-doubt perceptions.

We may never discover the root cause of the unconscious forces behind our destructive habits and behaviours but that does not stop us from both accepting our shadows and working to replace negativity as our default setting (unconscious) by changing that setting with new positive programming through first our conscious beliefs and intentions then through repetition becoming our new positive programming. It is a simple purpose in life to transcend what came before, to get better, this will be achieved by self-mastery of our minds and consequently our bodies. Accepting bodymind as one. A process that begins now and progresses through every precious moment.

"Everything is energy
and that is all
there is to it.
Match the frequency
of the reality you want
and you cannot help
but get that reality.
It can be no other way.
This is not philosophy.
This is physics"

~Albert Einstein~

 **Conclusion**

It seems to be human nature to need to envisage a destination, a goal or some kind of target as the aim of life. It is my thought at this time that awareness, progress and getting better have no ultimate goal or prize to be attained and that each day, each moment in fact contains within it the seed that is the richness of human experience we all crave, if only we could be present in our own lives we would be rewarded constantly. It is the asking of questions and the discovery of yet more questions that the soul needs more than answers or destinations of which there are none that can be named. Such questions trouble us into personal growth and progress. Precious moments presented to us each day, contained in every moment are the nuggets that we are searching for and all too often we have our eyes, minds and hearts set on an illusory prize or ultimate moment and miss the richness of the journey altogether – "Being happy when" we have met the perfect mate, have the ideal body, perfect car, home, holiday or night out but that never happens because our eyes, minds and hearts are always ahead of us imagining what could be or what is next on the list of stuff that will make us happy and provide peace of mind for life. Alas! It just never seems to hit the spot, maybe next time!

Life can only be lived in the now, in this moment right now. Are we missing our own lives? I know I still miss much of mine but I am working hard to be here for more of it.

This is the point when desire becomes suffering, when we cease to be present because something better is coming. When in reality that moment of anticipation is as good as it gets. We are conditioned to always look forward greedily to wanting shinier toys or defining moments that never live up to our expectations and are transitory and gone before we know it even when we still have the object of our desires the shine wears off. We are brainwashed into giving away our lives for the promise of something better that consumes our precious moments from the moment the seed is planted. Then at our leisure we look back with fondness and often regret to the moments we gave up. Where did the time go? We wish we had appreciated those moments more with every pore of our being. Sod the pictures! We want those moments inside of us forever as part of who we are. Looking back at the people and pets that I have lost without fail I feel I should have known them better and it is not physical pictures that I cherish but rather small moments, the living images in my mind that endure and that I value. Images that arise without planning or effort. Moments that are triggered by other such precious moments linked together for eternity and ready to rise to consciousness with perfect timing.

We become too busy wanting what we are told is important to our lives. A poor trade off. It is worth remembering that it is not how things are that is important but how we look at them that diminishes or enriches our lives. Learning to value what we have and not valuing what we don't have is a good start.

So where does that leave us when we are asking how best to live our lives? The first thing to accept is that non-stop happiness is an unobtainable and quite frankly ridiculous goal. Without the opposite of sadness happiness would have no meaning and our greatest learning experiences come from moments of adversity. There is very little growth to be had from happy moments. It is neither practical or realistic to have happiness as your main goal or priority in life. Happy happens if you just let it happen naturally and accept it's polar opposite of sadness.

Happiness is used to control us through corporations and politicians promising exactly that with their "best for us" products and decisions backed by convenient science and bull shitting experts. How is that working out for us so far? They really must think us foolish animals to constantly fall for the same lies repackaged and to pay for the privilege with our hard earned money. The first point is stop chasing endless happiness, life is a balancing of opposites.

The second point that we can work on is accepting that currently our minds are trained to dwell on what we don't have, not what we do have and in the realm of having in general. Also our minds dwell on where we are not rather than where we are. The result is a mind full of irrelevant (to our lives now), petty concerns and distractions. We have become unable to be present in our real life given situations. Our minds roam between the past and the future, barely noticing the present moment. Consequently, we never experience anything fully without distraction or to use the current word for this phenomena, mindfully. Our whole life becomes one of split attention, multi-tasking and inner turbulence. Rarely doing any one thing alone and mindfully. Mindfulness has arisen as the opposite of multi-tasking, maybe, as is common with opposites there is a balance to be found somewhere in the middle ground. Our minds take us away from what we should be enjoying. We may be physically present but elsewhere in mind.

Much of our time is spent wanting but what we have is never any good and what we don't have is absolutely marvellous and we simply can't live without it. Even though that is the way we felt about what we have now, it is no longer worth wanting for various extremely dubious reasons.

We are mind controlled to be this way so we can play the perfect consumer for our entire lives and more importantly to distract us away from ever looking at what goes on behind our backs. We live in a world that is fed to us to keep us docile. It is that simple.

The second point here again is quite simple but not easy to achieve. I think it is possible to regain control of our minds and appreciate what we have and every present moment. Eliminate any suspected mind control mechanisms from our lives and I would imagine there are many that as yet we are as yet oblivious to. For example, marketing advertisements, television "experts" wheeled in to sell us an idea and well-meaning friends that have bought into the crap. The time is ripe to live our own lives and no longer be that automaton created by an enslaving system that cares little or not at all for the masses other than how we can be manipulated best for their selfish interests by behaving predictably. A good place to start is by eliminating commercial television and the news from our lives and our families lives and then being mindful of the "real" suggestions behind any media to which we are exposed. The radio in our car is another source, we can easily just listen to music non-stop without all of the ads and suggestions that arise from those ads. I have a real issue with the gym that I use having commercial music television on constantly. Once we are aware of what is happening the suggestions become so obvious and the way many are worded is extremely devious. No wonder people are always ill. We are brainwashed to expect to be ill. Both whilst driving and whilst exercising we are often in trance states that are akin to hypnotic trance states. Our much trusted news media being one of the greatest mind control and propaganda devices to which we are exposed and we are particularly vulnerable due to our misplaced trust in its reliability and purpose of keeping us informed accurately and truthfully of what is happening around the world and locally. That is quite frankly laughable as fairy tales contain more truth. It always surprises me when a person in our service is caught lying and everybody is at first shocked and then accepts that it is a one off instance and the truth is prevalent in our governments. I think that getting the truth, the whole truth and nothing but the truth would be a one off and that lies and deceit is the default setting for world governments. We are oblivious to the motives behind our oppressor's actions.

The conclusion to this book 3 has to be that once aware the process of progressing and getting better is a lifetime purpose. At a time when we thought we would be coasting to the end of our lives we have an amazing unfinished journey to take on day by day, moment by moment. We can get better in our fitness, nutrition, relations with others, control of our own minds, losing attachments and addictions such as consumerism and eating, giving, loving, reading, understanding our psychology, our relationship with nature and the planet and the list goes on and on. Most of this by learning to know ourselves as we are really and not the act we put on for society and others.

Where to begin? I would suggest by beginning to make changes to lifestyle to include some of the above or other paths of progress. Personally I recommend that you begin to read some of the books I have included on my website www.adamsenex.com and choose a path that suits your unique personality and circumstances. I will continue to work on myself and I will continue to write about my life for better or worse. That way if you do feel stuck for ideas to act upon you can see what the crazy man is up to now. My next book (4) is titled *"Sometimes I pretend to be Normal"* and I will be including changes that I have made in my life that feel, to me, more suited to progress and getting better. I wish you the best of luck and thank you for taking the time out of your busy life to read my ramblings. Maybe together we can turn the ripples of change into a tidal wave that washes away the violence and deceit in this world.

Peace & Love

Adam Senex

Write to be understood, speak to be heard, READ TO GROW.

— Lawrence Clark Powell

VeryBestQuotes.com

Getting Better

Top Personal Development Books

www.adamsenex.com

Top Personal Development Blog @

www.MoreRebelThanZen.com

Life Coaching @ www.soul2whole.com

 ## Adam Senex – Getting Better Series

Book 1 – Dazed & Confused

Book 2 – More Rebel Than Zen

Book 3 – Chilled Demons Cheeky Heroes

Book 4 – Sometimes I Pretend To Be Normal

Book 5 – Coming Soon……..

also

The Great Body Bible - The Fitness Wizards available from www.authorhouse.co.uk

Feeding The Active Body - Gary Walsh

59289269R00117

Made in the USA
Charleston, SC
01 August 2016